Praise for C++ *Common Knowl*

"We live in a time when, perhaps surprisingly, the best printed works on C++ are just now emerging. This is one of those works. Although C++ has been at the forefront of innovation and productivity in software development for more than two decades, it is only now being fully understood and utilized. This book is one of those rare contributions that can bear repeated study by practitioners and experts alike. It is not a treatise on the arcane or academic—rather it completes your understanding of things you think you know but will bite you sooner or later until you *really* learn them. Few people have mastered C++ and software design as well as Steve has; almost no one has such a level head as he when it comes to software development. He knows what you need to know, believe me. When he speaks, I always listen—closely. I invite you to do the same. You (and your customers) will be glad you did."

—Chuck Allison, editor, *The C++ Source*

"Steve taught me C++. This was back in 1982 or 1983, I think—he had just returned from an internship sitting with Bjarne Stroustrup [inventor of C++] at Bell Labs. Steve is one of the unsung heroes of the early days, and anything Steve writes is on my A-list of things to read. This book is an easy read and collects a great deal of Steve's extensive knowledge and experience. It is highly recommended."

—Stan Lippman, coauthor of C++ *Primer, Fourth Edition*

"I welcome the self-consciously non-Dummies approach of a short, smart book."

—Matthew P. Johnson, Columbia University

"I agree with [the author's] assessment of the types of programmers. I have encountered the same types in my experience as a developer and a book like this will go far to help bridge their knowledge gap.... I think this book complements other books, like *Effective* C++ by Scott Meyers. It presents everything in a concise and easy-to-read style."

—Moataz Kamel, senior software designer, Motorola Canada

"Dewhurst has written yet another very good book. This book should be required reading for people who are using C++ (and think that they already know everything in C++)."

—Clovis Tondo, coauthor of C++ *Primer Answer Book*

C++ Common Knowledge

C++ Common Knowledge

Essential Intermediate Programming

Stephen C. Dewhurst

Addison-Wesley

Upper Saddle River, NJ • Boston • Indianapolis • San Francisco
New York • Toronto • Montreal • London • Munich • Paris • Madrid
Capetown • Sydney • Tokyo • Singapore • Mexico City

The publisher offers excellent discounts on this book when ordered in quantity for bulk purchases or special sales, which may include electronic versions and/or custom covers and content particular to your business, training goals, marketing focus, and branding interests. For more information, please contact:

U. S. Corporate and Government Sales
(800) 382-3419
corpsales@pearsontechgroup.com

For sales outside of the U. S., please contact:

International Sales
international@pearsoned.com

Visit us on the Web: www.awprofessional.com

Library of Congress Cataloging-in-Publication Data:
Dewhurst, Stephen C.
C++ common knowledge : essential intermediate programming / Stephen C. Dewhurst.
p. cm.
Includes bibliographical references and index.
ISBN 0-321-32192-8 (pbk. : alk. paper)
1. C++ (Computer program language) I. Title.

QA76.73.C153D48797 2005
005.13'3—dc22

2004029089

ISBN 0-321-32192-8
Text printed in the United States on recycled paper at Courier in Stoughton, Massachusetts.
4th Printing October 2007

Contents

Preface

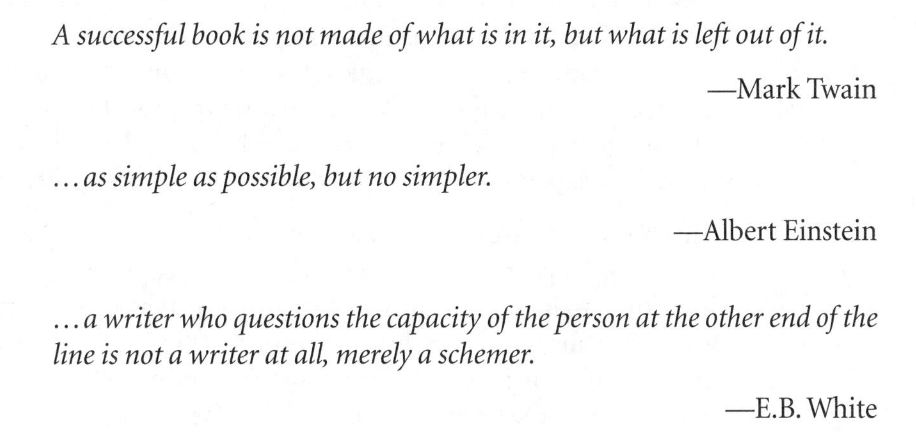

A successful book is not made of what is in it, but what is left out of it.

—Mark Twain

...as simple as possible, but no simpler.

—Albert Einstein

...a writer who questions the capacity of the person at the other end of the line is not a writer at all, merely a schemer.

—E.B. White

When he took over the editorship of the late *C++ Report*, the quick Herb Sutter asked me to write a column on a topic of my choosing. I agreed, and I chose to call the column "Common Knowledge." It was supposed to be, in Herb's words, "a regular summary of basic lore that every working C++ programmer should know—but can't always." After a couple of columns in that vein, however, I became interested in template metaprogramming techniques, and the topics treated in "Common Knowledge" from that point on were far from common.

However, the problem in the C++ programming industry that motivated my original choice of column remains. I commonly encounter the following types of individuals in my training and consulting work:

- Domain experts who are expert C programmers but who have only basic knowledge of (and perhaps some animosity toward) C++
- Talented new hires direct from university who have an academic appreciation for the C++ language but little production C++ experience

- Expert Java programmers who have little C++ experience and who have a tendency to program in C++ the way one would program in Java
- C++ programmers with several years of experience maintaining existing C++ applications but who have not been challenged to learn anything beyond the basics required for maintenance

I want to be immediately productive, but many of the people with whom I'm working or who I'm training require preliminary education in various C++ language features, patterns, and coding techniques before we can get down to business. Worse, I suspect that most C++ code is written in ignorance of at least some of these basics and is therefore not what most C++ experts would consider to be production quality.

This book addresses this pervasive problem by providing essential, common knowledge that every professional C++ programmer needs to know, in a form that is pared to its essentials and that can be efficiently and accurately absorbed. Much of the information is already available from other sources or is part of that compendium of unwritten information that all expert C++ programmers know. The advantage is that this material resides in one place and was selected according to what my training and consulting experience over many years has shown are the most commonly misunderstood and most useful language features, concepts, and techniques.

Perhaps the most important aspect of the sixty-three short items that make up this book is what they leave out, rather than what they contain. Many of these topics have the potential to become complex. An author's ignorance of these complexities could result in an uninformed description that could mislead the reader, but an expert discussion of a topic in its full complexity could inundate the reader. The approach used here is to filter out *needless* complexity in the discussion of each topic. What remains, I hope, is a clear distillation of the essentials required for production C++ programming. C++ language wonks will recognize, therefore, that I've left out discussion of some issues that are interesting and even important from a theoretical perspective, but the ignorance of which does not commonly affect one's ability to read and write production C++ code.

Another motivation for this book came as I was engaged in conversation with a group of well-known C++ experts at a conference. There was a general pall or depression among these experts that modern C++ is so complex that the "average" programmer can no longer understand it. (The specific issue was name binding in the context of templates and namespaces. Yes, getting worked up about such a topic does imply the need for more play with normal children.) On reflection, I'd have to say our attitude was pretentious and our gloom unwarranted. We "experts" have no such problems, and it's as easy to program in C++ as it is to speak a (vastly more complex) natural language, even if you can't diagram the deep structure of your every utterance. A recurring theme of this book is that while the full description of the minutia of a particular language feature may be daunting, day-to-day use of the feature is straightforward and natural.

Consider function overloading. A full description occupies a large chunk of the standard and whole or multiple chapters in many C++ texts. And yet, when faced with

```
void f( int );
void f( const char * );
//...
f( "Hello" );
```

not a single practicing C++ programmer will be unable to determine which `f` is called. Full knowledge of the rules by which a call to an overloaded function is resolved is useful but only rarely necessary. The same applies to many other ostensibly complex areas of C++ language and idiom.

This is not to say that all the material presented here is easy; it's "as simple as possible, but no simpler." In C++ programming, as in any other worthwhile intellectual activity, many important details can't be written on an index card. Moreover, this is not a book for "dummies." I feel a great deal of responsibility to those who grant a portion of their valuable time to reading my books. I respect these readers and try to communicate with them as I would in person to any of my colleagues. Writing at an eighth-grade level to a professional isn't writing. It's pandering.

Many of the book's items treat simple misunderstandings that I've seen over and over again, which just need to be pointed out (for example, scope order for member function lookup and the difference between overriding and overloading). Others deal with topics that are in the process of becoming essential knowledge for C++ professionals but are often incorrectly assumed to be difficult and are avoided (for example, class template partial specialization and template template parameters). I've received some criticism from the expert reviewers of the manuscript that I've spent too much space (approximately one third of the book) on template issues that are not really common knowledge. However, each of these experts pointed out one, two, or several of the template topics they thought did belong in the book. The telling observation is, I think, that there was little overlap among these suggestions, and every template-related item had at least one supporter.

This is the crux of the issue with the items that make up this book. I don't expect any reader to be ignorant of every item's topic, and it's likely that some readers will be familiar with all of them. Obviously, if a reader is not familiar with a particular topic, there would be (I presume) some benefit in reading about it. However, even if a reader is already familiar with a topic, I'd hope that reading about it from a new perspective might clear up a slight misunderstanding or lead to a deeper understanding. This book may also have a role in saving the more experienced C++ programmer precious time. Competent C++ programmers often find themselves (as described previously) answering the same questions over and over again to the detriment of their own work. I'd suggest that the approach of "read this first, and *then* let's talk" would save these C++ gurus countless hours and direct their expertise instead to the complex problems for which it's really needed.

I initially tried to group these sixty-three items into neat chapters, but the items had other ideas. They instead tended to clump themselves together in ways that ranged from the obvious to the unexpected. For example, the items related to exceptions and resource management form a rather natural group. Less obviously, the items *Capability Queries*, *Meaning of Pointer* Comparison, *Virtual Constructors and Prototype*, *Factory Method*, and *Covariant Return Types* are strongly and somewhat surprisingly interrelated and are best grouped in close proximity to each other. *Pointer Arithmetic* decided to hang with *Smart Pointers* rather than with the pointer and array material earlier in the book. Rather than attempt to impose an arbitrary chapter structure on these natural groupings, I decided to grant the individual items freedom of association. Of course, many other interrelationships exist among the topics treated by the items than can be represented in a simple linear ordering, so the items make frequent internal references among themselves. It's a clumped but connected community.

While the main idea is to be brief, discussion of a topic sometimes includes ancillary details that are not directly related to the subject at hand. These details are never necessary to follow the discussion, but the reader is put on notice that a particular facility or technique exists. For instance, the `Heap` template example that appears in several items informs the reader in passing about the existence of the useful but rarely discussed STL heap algorithms, and the discussion of placement new outlines the technical basis of the sophisticated buffer management techniques employed by much of the standard library. I also try to take the opportunity, whenever it seems natural to do so, to fold the discussion of subsidiary topics into the discussion of a particular, named item. Therefore, *RAII* contains a short discussion of the order of constructor and destructor activation, *Template Argument Deduction* discusses the use of helper functions for specializing class templates, and *Assignment and Initialization Are Different* folds in a discussion of computational constructors. This book could easily have twice the number of items, but, like the clumping of the items themselves, correlation of a subsidiary topic with a specific item puts the topic in context and helps the reader to absorb the material efficiently and accurately.

I've reluctantly included several topics that cannot reasonably be treated in this book's format of short items. In particular, the items on design patterns and the design of the standard template library are laughably short and incomplete. Yet they make an appearance simply to put some common misconceptions to rest, emphasize the importance of the topics, and encourage the reader to learn more.

Stock examples are part of our programming culture, like the stories that families swap when they gather for holidays. Therefore, `Shape`, `String`, `Stack`, and many of the other usual suspects put in an appearance. The common appreciation of these baseline examples confers the same efficiencies as design patterns in communication, as in "Suppose I want to rotate a `Shape`, except..." or "When you concatenate two `Strings`..." Simply mentioning a common example orients the conversation and avoids the need for time-consuming background discussion. "You know how your brother acts whenever he's arrested? Well, the other day..."

Unlike my previous books, this one tries to avoid passing judgment on certain poor programming practices and misuses of C++ language features; that's a goal for other books, the best of which I list in the bibliography. (I was, however, not entirely successful in avoiding the tendency to preach; some bad programming practices just have to be mentioned, even if only in passing.) The goal of this book is to inform the reader of the technical essentials of production-level C++ programming in as efficient a manner as possible.

—Stephen C. Dewhurst
Carver, Massachusetts
January 2005

Acknowledgments

Peter Gordon, editor *on ne peut plus extraordinaire*, withstood my kvetching about the state of education in the C++ community for an admirably long time before suggesting that I do something about it. This book is the result. Kim Boedigheimer somehow managed to keep the entire project on track without even once making violent threats to the author.

The expert technical reviewers—Matthew Johnson, Moataz Kamel, Dan Saks, Clovis Tondo, and Matthew Wilson—pointed out several errors and many infelicities of language in the manuscript, helping to make this a better book. A stubborn individual, I haven't followed *all* their recommendations, so any errors or infelicities that remain are entirely my fault.

Some of the material in this book appeared, in slightly different form, in my "Common Knowledge" column for *C/C++ Users Journal*, and much of the material appeared in the "Once, Weakly" Web column on semantics.org. I received many insightful comments on both print and Web articles from Chuck Allison, Attila Fehér, Kevlin Henney, Thorsten Ottosen, Dan Saks, Terje Slettebø, Herb Sutter, and Leor Zolman. Several in-depth discussions with Dan Saks improved my understanding of the difference between template specialization and instantiation and helped me clarify the distinction between overloading and the appearance of overloading under ADL and infix operator lookup.

This book relies on less direct contributions as well. I'm indebted to Brandon Goldfedder for the algorithm analogy to patterns that appears in the item on design patterns and to Clovis Tondo both for motivation and for his assistance in finding qualified reviewers. I've had the good fortune over the years to teach courses based on Scott Meyers's *Effective C++*, *More Effective C++*, and *Effective STL* books. This has allowed me to observe firsthand what background information was commonly missing from students who wanted to profit from these industry-standard, intermediate-level C++ books, and those observations have helped to shape the set of topics treated in this book. Andrei Alexandrescu's work inspired me to experiment with template metaprogramming rather than do what I was supposed to be doing, and both Herb Sutter's and Jack Reeves's work with exceptions has helped me to understand better how exceptions should be employed.

I'd also like to thank my neighbors and good friends Dick and Judy Ward, who periodically ordered me away from my computer to work the local cranberry harvest. For one whose professional work deals primarily in simplified abstractions of reality, it's intellectually healthful to be shown that the complexity involved in convincing a cranberry vine to bear fruit is a match for anything a C++ programmer may attempt with template partial specialization.

Sarah G. Hewins and David R. Dewhurst provided, as always, both valuable assistance and important impediments to this project.

I like to think of myself as a quiet person of steady habits, given more to calm reflection than strident demand. However, like those who undergo a personality transformation once they're behind the wheel of an automobile, when I get behind a manuscript I become a different person altogether. Addison-Wesley's terrific team of behavior modification professionals saw me through these personality issues. Chanda Leary-Coutu worked with Peter Gordon and Kim Boedigheimer to translate my rantings into rational business proposals and shepherd them through the powers-that-be. Molly Sharp and Julie Nahil not only turned an awkward word document into the graceful pages you see before you, they managed to correct many flaws in the manuscript while allowing me to retain my archaic sentence structure, unusual diction, and idiosyncratic hyphenation. In spite of my constantly changing requests, Richard Evans managed to stick to the schedule and produce not one, but two separate indexes. Chuti Prasertsith designed a gorgeous, cranberry-themed cover. Many thanks to all.

A Note on Typographical Conventions

As mentioned in the preface, these items frequently reference one another. Rather than simply mention the item number, which would force an examination of the table of contents to determine just what was being referenced, the title of the item is italicized and rendered in full. To permit easy reference to the item, the item number and page on which it appears are appended as subscripts. For example, the item referenced *Eat Your Vegetables* [64, 256] tells us that the item entitled "Eat Your Vegetables" is item 64, which can be found on page 256.

Code examples appear in fixed-width font to better distinguish them from the running text. Incorrect or inadvisable code examples appear with a gray background, and correct and proper code appears with no background.

Item 1 Data Abstraction

A "type" is a set of operations, and an "abstract data type" is a set of operations with an implementation. When we identify objects in a problem domain, the first question we should ask about them is, "What can I do with this object?" not "How is this object implemented?" Therefore, if a natural description of a problem involves employees, contracts, and payroll records, then the programming language used to solve the problem should contain `Employee`, `Contract`, and `PayrollRecord` types. This allows an efficient, two-way translation between the problem domain and the solution domain, and software written this way has less "translation noise" and is simpler and more correct.

In a general-purpose programming language like C++, we don't have application-specific types like `Employee`. Instead, we have something better: the language facilities to create sophisticated abstract data types. The purpose of an abstract data type is, essentially, to extend the programming language into a particular problem domain.

No universally accepted procedure exists for designing abstract data types in C++. This aspect of programming still has its share of inspiration and artistry, but most successful approaches follow a set of similar steps.

1. Choose a descriptive name for the type. If you have trouble choosing a name for the type, you don't know enough about what you want to implement. Go think some more. An abstract data type should represent a single, well-defined concept, and the name for that concept should be obvious.
2. List the operations that the type can perform. An abstract data type is defined by what you can do with it. Remember initialization (constructors), cleanup (destructor), copying (copy operations), and conversions (nonexplicit single-argument constructors and conversion operators). Never, ever, simply provide a bunch of get/set operations on the data members of the implementation. That's not data abstraction; that's laziness and lack of imagination.
3. Design an interface for the type. The type should be, as Scott Meyers tells us, "easy to use correctly and hard to use incorrectly." An

abstract data type extends the language; do proper language design. Put yourself in the place of the user of your type, and write some code with your interface. Proper interface design is as much a question of psychology and empathy as technical prowess.

4. Implement the type. Don't let the implementation affect the interface of the type. Implement the contract promised by the type's interface. Remember that the implementations of most abstract data types will change much more frequently than their interfaces.

Item 2 Polymorphism

The topic of polymorphism is given mystical status in some programming texts and is ignored in others, but it's a simple, useful concept that the C++ language supports. According to the standard, a "polymorphic type" is a class type that has a virtual function. From the design perspective, a "polymorphic object" is an object with more than one type, and a "polymorphic base class" is a base class that is designed for use by polymorphic objects.

Consider a type of financial option, `AmOption`, as shown in Figure 1.

An `AmOption` object has four types: It is simultaneously an `AmOption`, an `Option`, a `Deal`, and a `Priceable`. Because a type is a set of operations (see *Data Abstraction* [1, 1] and *Capability Queries* [27, 93]), an `AmOption` object can be manipulated through any one of its four interfaces. This means that an `AmOption` object can be manipulated by code that is written to the `Deal`, `Priceable`, and `Option` interfaces, thereby allowing the implementation of `AmOption` to leverage and reuse all that code. For a polymorphic type such as `AmOption`, the most important things inherited from its base classes are their interfaces, not their implementations. In

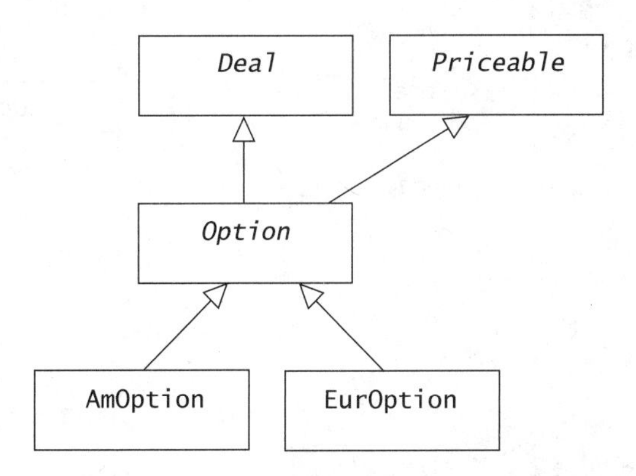

Figure 1 Polymorphic leveraging in a financial option hierarchy. An American option has four types.

fact, it's not uncommon, and is often desirable, for a base class to consist of nothing but interface (see *Capability Queries* [27, 93]).

Of course, there's a catch. For this leveraging to work, a properly designed polymorphic class must be substitutable for each of its base classes. In other words, if generic code written to the `Option` interface gets an `AmOption` object, that object had better behave like an `Option`!

This is not to say that an `AmOption` should behave identically to an `Option`. (For one thing, it may be the case that many of the `Option` base class's operations are pure virtual functions with no implementation.) Rather, it's profitable to think of a polymorphic base class like `Option` as a contract. The base class makes certain promises to users of its interface; these include firm syntactic promises that certain member functions can be called with certain types of arguments and less easily verifiable semantic promises concerning what will actually occur when a particular member function is called. Concrete derived classes like `AmOption` and `EurOption` are subcontractors that implement the contract `Option` has established with its clients, as shown in Figure 2.

For example, if `Option` has a pure virtual `price` member function that gives the present value of the `Option`, both `AmOption` and `EurOption` must implement this function. It obviously won't implement identical behavior for these two types of `Option`, but it should calculate and return a price, not make a telephone call or print a file.

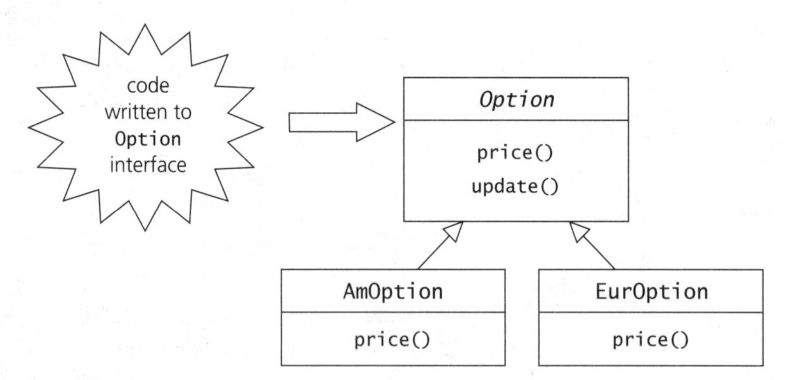

Figure 2 | A polymorphic contractor and its subcontractors. The `Option` base class specifies a contract.

On the other hand, if I were to call the `price` function of two different interfaces to the *same* object, I'd better get the same result. Essentially, either call should bind to the same function:

```
AmOption *d = new AmOption;
Option *b = d;
d->price(); // if this calls AmOption::price...
b->price(); // ...so should this!
```

This makes sense. (It's surprising how much of advanced object-oriented programming is basic common sense surrounded by impenetrable syntax.) If I were to ask you, "What's the present value of that American option?" I'd expect to receive the same answer if I'd phrased my question as, "What's the present value of that option?"

The same reasoning applies, of course, to an object's nonvirtual functions:

```
b->update(); // if this calls Option::update...
d->update(); // ...so should this!
```

The contract provided by the base class is what allows the "polymorphic" code written to the base class interface to work with specific options while promoting healthful ignorance of their existence. In other words, the polymorphic code may be manipulating `AmOption` and `EurOption` objects, but as far as it's concerned they're all just `Options`. Various concrete `Option` types can be added and removed without affecting the generic code that is aware only of the `Option` base class. If an `AsianOption` shows up at some point, the polymorphic code that knows only about `Options` will be able to manipulate it in blissful ignorance of its specific type, and if it should later disappear, it won't be missed.

By the same token, concrete option types such as `AmOption` and `EurOption` need to be aware only of the base classes whose contracts they implement and are independent of changes to the generic code. In principle, the base class can be ignorant of everything but itself. From a practical perspective, the design of its interface will take into account the requirements of its anticipated users, and it should be designed in such a way that derived classes can easily deduce and implement its contract (see *Template Method* [22, 77]). However, a base class should have no specific knowledge of any of the classes derived from it, because such knowledge inevitably makes it difficult to add or remove derived classes in the hierarchy.

In object-oriented design, as in life, ignorance is bliss (see also *Virtual Constructors and Prototype* [29, 99] and *Factory Method* [30, 103]).

Item 3 | Design Patterns

Anyone who is not already familiar with design patterns may, after a brief survey of the field, come away with the impression that design patterns are a lot of marketing hype, are just some simple coding techniques, or are the playthings of computer scientists who really should get out more. While each of these impressions carries a grain of truth, design patterns are an essential component of the professional C++ programmer's toolkit.

A "design pattern" is a recurring architectural theme that provides a solution to a common design problem within a particular context and describes the consequences of this solution. A design pattern is more than a simple description of a technique; it's a named capsule of design wisdom gleaned from successful existing practice, written in such a way that it can be easily communicated and reused. Patterns are about programmer to programmer communication.

From a practical perspective, design patterns have two important properties. First, they describe proven, successful design techniques that can be customized in a context-dependent way to new design situations. Second, and perhaps more important, mentioning the application of a particular pattern serves to document not only the technique that is applied but also the reasons for its application and the effect of having applied it.

This sort of thing is nothing new. Consider an analogy from the field of algorithms. (Algorithms are not design patterns, and they're not "code patterns." They're algorithms, and this is an analogy.) Consider the following statement that I might make to a colleague: "I have an unsorted sequence that I have to search a number of times. Therefore, I'm going to quick sort it and use binary search to perform each lookup." The ability to use the terms "quick sort" and "binary search" is of inestimable value not only in design but also in communicating that design to an educated colleague. When I say "quick sort," my colleague knows that the sequence I'm sorting is in a random access structure, that it will probably be sorted within $O(nlg_2n)$ time, and that the elements in the sequence may be compared with a less-than-like operator. When I say "binary search," my colleague knows (even if I hadn't earlier mentioned "quick sort") that the sequence is sorted, that I will locate the item of interest within $O(\lg_2 n)$ comparisons, and that an appropriate operation is available to compare sequence elements. Shared knowledge of, and a standard vocabulary for, standard algorithms permits not only efficient documentation but also efficient criticism. For example, if I planned to perform this search and sort procedure on a singly linked list structure, my colleague would immediately smirk and point out that I couldn't use quick sort and probably wouldn't want to use binary search.

Until the advent of design patterns, we missed these advantages in documentation, communication, and efficient smirking with our object-oriented designs. We were forced into low-level descriptions of our designs, with all the inefficiency and imprecision that entails. It's not that techniques for sophisticated object-oriented design didn't exist; it's that the techniques were not readily available to the entire programming community under a shared, common terminology. Design patterns address that problem, and we can now describe object-oriented designs as efficiently and unambiguously as algorithmic designs.

For example, when we see that the Bridge pattern has been applied to a design, we know that at a simple mechanical level an abstract data type implementation has been separated into an interface class and an implementation class. Additionally, we know that the reason this was done was to separate strongly the interface from the implementation so that changes to the implementation would not affect users of the interface. We also know a runtime cost exists for this separation, how the source code for the abstract data type should be arranged, and many other details. A pattern name is an efficient, unambiguous handle to a wealth of information and experience about a technique, and careful, accurate use of patterns and pattern terminology in design and documentation clarifies code and designs.

Patterns wonks sometimes describe design patterns as a form of literature (they really do) that follows a certain formal structure. Several common variants are in use, but all forms contain four essential parts.

First, a design pattern must have an unambiguous name. For example, the term "wrapper" is useless for a design pattern, because it is already in common use and has dozens of meanings. Using a term like "Wrapper" as a pattern name would lead only to confusion and misunderstanding.

Instead, the different design techniques that formerly went under the name "wrapper" are now designated by the pattern names "Bridge," "Strategy," "Façade," "Object Adapter," and probably several others. Use of a precise pattern name has a clear advantage over using a less precise term, in the same way that "binary search" is a more precise and useful term than "lookup."

Second, the pattern description must define the problem addressed by the pattern. This description may be relatively broad or narrow.

Third, the pattern description describes the problem's solution. Depending on the statement of the problem, the solution may be rather high level or relatively low level, but it should still be general enough to customize according to the various contexts in which the problem may occur.

Fourth, the pattern description describes the consequences of applying the pattern to the context. How has the context changed for better or worse after application of the pattern?

Will knowledge of patterns make a bad designer a good designer? Time for another analogy: Consider one of those painful mathematics courses you may have been forced to undergo, in which the final examination is to prove a number of theorems in a certain area of mathematics. How do you get out of such a course alive? One obvious way is to be a genius. Starting from first principles, you develop the underpinnings of an entire branch of mathematics and eventually prove the theorems. A more practical approach would be to memorize and internalize a large number of theorems in that area of mathematics and use whatever native mathematical ability, inspiration, or good luck you have at your disposal to select the appropriate subsidiary theorems and combine them with some logical glue to prove the new theorems. This approach is advantageous even for our fictitious genius, because a proof built upon established theorems is more efficient to construct and easier to communicate to mere mortals. Familiarity with subsidiary theorems does not, of course, guarantee that a poor mathematician will be able to pass the test, but such knowledge will at least enable that person to understand the proof once it has been produced.

In a similar vein, developing a complex object-oriented design from first principles is probably going to be tedious, and communication of the eventual design difficult. Composition of design patterns to produce an object-oriented design is similar to use of subsidiary theorems in mathematics to prove a new theorem. Design patterns are often described as "micro-architectures" that can be composed with other patterns to produce a new architecture. Of course, selecting appropriate patterns and composing them effectively requires design expertise and native ability. However, even your manager will be able to understand the completed design if he or she has the requisite knowledge of patterns.

Item 4 The Standard Template Library

A short description of the standard template library (STL) cannot do its design justice. What follows is an appetizer to encourage you to study the STL in depth.

The STL isn't really a library. It's an inspired idea and a set of conventions.

The STL consists of three major kinds of components: containers, algorithms, and iterators. Containers contain and organize elements. Algorithms perform operations. Iterators are used to access the elements of a container. This is nothing new, as many traditional libraries have these components, and many traditional libraries are implemented with templates. The STL's inspired idea is that containers and the algorithms that operate on them need no knowledge of each other. This sleight of hand is accomplished with iterators.

An iterator is like a pointer. (In fact, pointers are one kind of STL iterator.) Like a pointer, an iterator can refer to an element of a sequence, can be dereferenced to get the value of the object to which it refers, and can be manipulated like a pointer to refer to different elements of a sequence. STL iterators may be predefined pointers, or they may be user-defined class types that overload the appropriate operators to have the same syntax of use as a predefined pointer (see *Smart Pointers* [42, 145]).

An STL container is an abstraction of a data structure, implemented as a class template. As with different data structures, different containers organize their elements in different ways to optimize access or manipulation. The STL defines seven (or, if you count `string`, eight) standard containers, and several widely accepted nonstandard containers are available.

An STL algorithm is an abstraction of a function, implemented as a function template (see *Generic Algorithms* [60, 221]). Most STL algorithms work with one or more sequences of values, where a sequence is defined by an ordered pair of iterators. The first iterator refers to the first element of the sequence, and the second iterator refers to one past the last element of the sequence (*not* to the last element). If the iterators refer to the same location, they define an empty sequence.

Iterators are the mechanism by which containers and algorithms work together. A container can produce a pair of iterators that indicates a sequence of its elements (either all its elements or a subrange), and an algorithm operates on that sequence. In this way, containers and algorithms can work closely together while remaining ignorant of each other. (The beneficial effect of ignorance is a recurring theme in advanced C++ programming. See *Polymorphism* [2, 3], *Factory Method* [30, 103], *Commands and Hollywood* [19, 67], and *Generic Algorithms* [60, 221].)

In addition to containers, algorithms, and iterators, the STL defines a number of ancillary capabilities. Algorithms and containers may be customized with function pointers and function objects (see *STL Function Objects* [20, 71]), and these function objects may be adapted and combined with various function object adapters.

Containers may also be adapted with container adapters that modify the interface of the container to be that of a stack, queue, or priority queue.

The STL relies heavily on convention. Containers and function objects must describe themselves through a standard set of nested type names (see *Embedded Type Information* [53, 189], *Traits* [54, 193], and *STL Function Objects* [20, 71]). Both container and function object adapters require that member functions have specific names and contain specific type information. Algorithms require that iterators passed to them be able to support certain operations and be able to identify what these operations are. If you abandon convention when using or extending the STL, abandon all hope as well. If you adhere to convention when using the STL, you'll have an easy life.

The STL conventions do not specify implementation details, but they do specify efficiency constraints on the implementation. In addition, because the STL is a template library, much optimization and tuning can take place at compile time. Many of the naming and information conventions mentioned previously are there precisely to allow significant compile-time optimization. Use of the STL generally rivals the efficiency of hand-coding by an expert, and it beats hand-coding by the average nonexpert or by any team of programmers hands down. The result is also generally clearer and more maintainable.

Learn the STL, and use it extensively.

Item 5 | References Are Aliases, Not Pointers

A reference is another name for an existing object. Once a reference is initialized with an object, either the object name or the reference name may be used to refer to the object.

```
int a = 12;
int &ra = a; // ra is another name for a
--ra; // a == 11
a = 10; // ra == 10
int *ip = &ra; // ip points to a
```

References are often confused with pointers, perhaps because C++ compilers often implement references as pointers, but they are not pointers and do not behave like pointers.

Three major differences between references and pointers are that there are no null references, all references require initialization, and a reference always refers to the object with which it is initialized. In the previous example, the reference `ra` will refer to `a` for its entire lifetime. Most erroneous uses of references stem from misunderstanding these differences.

Some compilers may catch an obvious attempt to create a null reference:

```
Employee &anEmployee = *static_cast<Employee*>(0); // error!
```

However, the compiler may not detect less obvious attempts to create a null reference, which will cause undefined behavior at runtime:

```
Employee *getAnEmployee();
//...
Employee &anEmployee = *getAnEmployee(); // probably bad code
if( &anEmployee == 0 ) // undefined behavior
```

If getAnEmployee returns a null pointer, then the behavior of this code is undefined. In this case, it's better to use a pointer to hold the result of getAnEmployee.

```
Employee *employee = getAnEmployee();
if( employee ) //...
```

The requirement that a reference must be initialized implies that the object to which it refers must be in existence when the reference is initialized. This is important, so I'll say it again: A reference is an alias for an object that already exists prior to the initialization of the reference. Once a reference is initialized to refer to a particular object, it cannot later be made to refer to a different object; a reference is bound to its initializer for its whole lifetime. In effect, after initialization a reference disappears and is simply another name for its initializer thereafter. This aliasing property is why references are often a good choice for function formal arguments; in the following swap template function, the formal arguments a and b become aliases for the actual arguments to the call:

```
template <typename T>
void swap( T &a, T &b ) {
    T temp(a);
    a = b;
    b = temp;
}
//...
int x = 1, y = 2;
swap( x, y ); // x == 2, y == 1
```

In the call to swap above, a aliases x, and b aliases y, for the duration of the call. Note that the object to which a reference refers needn't have a name, so a reference may be used to give a convenient name to an unnamed object:

```
int grades[MAX];
//...
swap( grades[i], grades[j] );
```

After the formal arguments a and b of swap are initialized with the actual arguments grades[i] and grades[j], respectively, those two nameless array elements can be manipulated through the aliases a and b. This property may be used more directly in order to simplify and optimize.

Consider the following function that sets a particular element of a two-dimensional array:

```
inline void set_2d( float *a, int m, int i, int j ) {
    a[i*m+j] = a[i*m+j] * a[i*m+i] + a[i*m+j]; // oops!
}
```

We can replace the line commented "oops!" with a simpler version that employs a reference and that has the additional advantage of being correct. (Did you catch the error? I didn't the first time around.)

```
inline void set_2d( float *a, int m, int i, int j ) {
    float &r = a[i*m+j];
    r = r * r + r;
}
```

A reference to a non-const cannot be initialized with a literal or temporary value.

```
double &d = 12.3; // error!
swap( std::string("Hello"), std::string(", World") ); // errors!
```

However, a reference to const can:

```
const double &cd = 12.3; // OK
template <typename T>
T add( const T &a, const T &b ) {
    return a + b;
}
//...
const std::string &greeting
    = add(std::string("Hello"),std::string(", World")); // OK
```

When a reference to const is initialized with a literal, the reference is set to refer to a temporary location that is initialized with the literal. Therefore, `cd` does not actually refer to the literal `12.3` but to a temporary of type `double` that has been initialized with `12.3`. The reference `greeting` refers to the unnamed temporary `string` return value of the call to `add`. Ordinarily, such temporaries are destroyed (that is, go out of scope and have their destructors called) at the end of the expression in which they're created. However, when such a temporary is used to initialize a reference to const, the temporary will exist as long as the reference that refers to it.

Item 6 | Array Formal Arguments

Array formal arguments are problematic. The major surprise in store for the C/C++ novice is that there are no array formal arguments, because an array is passed as a pointer to its first element.

```
void average( int ary[12] ); // formal arg is int *
//...
int anArray[] = { 1, 2, 3 }; // three-element array
const int anArraySize =
    sizeof(anArray)/sizeof(anArray[0]); // == 3
average( anArray ); // legal!
```

This automatic transformation from array to pointer is given the charming technical term "decay"; an array decays to a pointer to its first element. The same thing happens to functions, by the way. A function argument decays to a pointer to a function, but, unlike an array that loses its bound, a decaying function has the good sense to hold onto its argument and return types. (Note also the proper compile-time calculation of `anArraySize` that can withstand changes both to the set of initializers of the array and to the array's element type.)

Because the array bound is ignored in an array formal argument, it's usually best to omit it. However, if the function is expecting a pointer to a sequence of elements (that is, an array) as an argument, rather than a pointer to a single object, then it's probably best to say so:

```
void average( int ary[] ); // formal arg is still int *
```

If, on the other hand, the precise value of the array bound is important, and you want the function to accept only arrays with a particular number of elements, you may consider a reference formal argument:

```
void average( int (&ary)[12] );
```

Now our function will accept only integer arrays of size 12.

```
average( anArray ); // error! anArray is int [3]!
```

Templates can help to generalize somewhat,

```
template <int n>
void average( int (&ary)[n] ); // let compiler deduce n for us
```

but a more traditional solution is to pass the size of the array explicitly.

```
void average_n( int ary[], int size );
```

Of course, we can combine the two approaches:

```
template <int n>
inline void average( int (&ary)[n] )
    { average_n( ary, n ); }
```

It should be clear from this discussion that one of the major problems with using arrays as function arguments is that the size of the array must be encoded explicitly in the type of the formal argument, passed as a separate argument, or indicated by a "terminator" value within the array itself (such as the `'\0'` that is used to indicate the end of a character array used as a string). Another difficulty is that—no matter how it is declared—an array is often manipulated through a pointer to its first element. If that pointer is passed as the actual argument to a function, our previous trick of declaring a reference formal argument will not help us.

```
int *anArray2 = new int[anArraySize];
//...
average( anArray2 ); // error! can't init int(&)[n] with int *
average_n( anArray, anArraySize ); // OK...
```

For these reasons, one of the standard containers (typically `vector` or `string`) is often a good substitute for most traditional uses of arrays and should generally be considered first. See also the `Array` class template in *You Instantiate What You Use* [61, 225].

Multidimensional array formal arguments are not essentially more difficult than simple arrays, but they look more challenging:

```
void process( int ary[10][20] );
```

As in the single-dimensional case, the formal argument is not an array but a pointer to the array's first element. However, a multidimensional array is an array of arrays, so the formal argument is a pointer to an array (see *Dealing with Function and Array Declarators* [17, 61] and *Pointer Arithmetic* [44, 149]).

```
void process( int (*ary)[20] ); // ptr to array of 20 ints
```

Note that the second (and subsequent) bounds are not decayed, because otherwise it would not be possible to perform pointer arithmetic with the formal argument (see *Pointer Arithmetic* [44, 149]). As noted previously, it's often a good idea to let your reader know you expect the actual argument to be an array:

```
void process( int ary[][20] ); // still a pointer, but clearer
```

Effective processing of multidimensional array arguments often decays into an exercise in low-level coding, with the programmer taking the compiler's place in performing index calculations:

```
void process_2d( int *a, int n, int m ) { // a is an n by m array
    for( int i = 0; i < n; ++i )
        for( int j = 0; j < m; ++j )
            a[i*m+j] = 0; // calculate index "by hand"!
}
```

As usual, a template can sometimes help to clean things up.

```
template <int n, int m>
inline void process( int (&ary)[n][m] )
    { process_2d( &ary[0][0], n, m ); }
```

Simply put, array formal arguments are a pain in the neck. Approach with caution.

Item 7 | Const Pointers and Pointers to Const

In casual conversation, C++ programmers will often say "const pointer" when they really mean "pointer to const." That's unfortunate, because these are two different concepts.

```
T *pt = new T; // ptr to T
const T *pct = pt; // ptr to const T
T *const cpt = pt; // const ptr to T
```

Before you start tossing `const` qualifiers into your pointer declarations, you first have to decide what it is that you want to be const: the pointer, the object to which you're pointing, or both. In the declaration of `pct`, the pointer is not const, but the object it points to is considered to be const; that is, the `const` qualifier modifies the `T` base type, not the `*` pointer modifier. In the case of `cpt`, we're declaring a constant pointer to a non-constant object; the `const` qualifier modifies the `*` pointer modifier, not the `T` base type.

To further confuse the syntactic issues surrounding pointers and `const`, the order of the declaration specifiers (that is, everything in the pointer declaration that occurs before the first `*` modifier) is immaterial. For instance, the following two declarations declare variables of exactly the same type:

```
const T *p1; // ptr to const T
T const *p2; // also ptr to const T
```

The first form is more traditional, but many C++ experts now recommend the second form. The reasoning is that the second form is less prone to misunderstanding because the declaration can be read backward, as in "pointer to constant `T`." It doesn't really matter which form we use as long as we're consistent. Be careful, however, of the common error of confusing a declaration of a const pointer with that of a pointer to const.

```
T const *p3; // ptr to const
T *const p4 = pt; // const ptr to non-const
```

It's possible, of course, to declare a const pointer to a const.

```
const T *const cpct1 = pt; // everything is const
T const *const cpct2 = cpct1; // same type
```

Note that it's often simpler to use a reference in preference to a const pointer:

```
const T &rct = *pt; // rather than const T *const
T &rt = *pt; // rather than T *const
```

Notice in some of the previous examples that we were able to convert a pointer to non-const into a pointer to const. For example, we were able to initialize `pct` (of type `const T *`) with the value of `pt` (of type `T *`). The reason this is legal is that, speaking nontechnically, nothing bad can happen. Consider what happens when the address of a non-const object is copied to a pointer to const, as shown in Figure 3.

The pointer to const `pct` is pointing to a non-const `T`, but that won't cause any harm. In fact, it's common to refer to non-constant objects with pointers (or references) to const:

```
void aFunc( const T *arg1, const T &arg2 );
//...
T *a = new T;
T b;
aFunc( a, b );
```

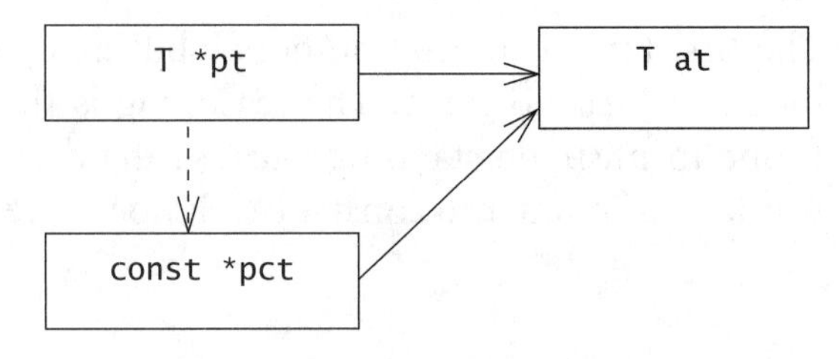

Figure 3 A pointer to const may refer to a non-const object.

When we call `aFunc`, we initialize `arg1` with `a` and `arg2` with `b`. We are not claiming thereby that `a` points to a const object or that `b` is a const; we are claiming that they will be treated as if they were const within `aFunc`, whether or not they actually are. Very useful.

The reverse conversion, from pointer to const to pointer to non-const, is not legal because it would be dangerous, as illustrated in Figure 4.

In this case, `pct` may actually be pointing to an object that was defined to be const. If we could convert a pointer to const to a pointer to non-const, then `pt` could be used to change the value of `acT`.

```
const T acT;
pct = &acT;
pt = pct; // error, fortunately
*pt = aT; // attempt to change const object!
```

The C++ standard tells us that such an assignment will have undefined results; we don't know precisely what will happen, but whatever it is won't be good. Of course, we can use a cast to perform the conversion explicitly.

```
pt = const_cast<T *>(pct); // not an error, but inadvisable
*pt = aT; // attempt to change const object!
```

However, the behavior of the assignment is still undefined if `pt` refers to an object that, like `acT`, was declared to be const (see *New Cast Operators* [9, 29]).

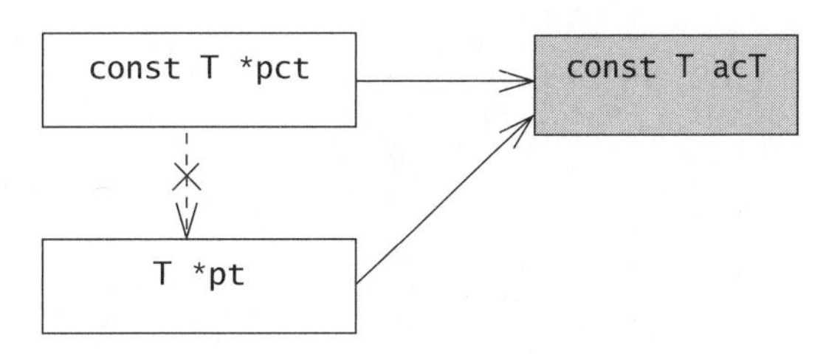

Figure 4 A pointer to non-const may not refer to a const object.

Item 8 | Pointers to Pointers

It's legal to declare a pointer to a pointer. This is what the C++ standard calls a "multilevel" pointer.

```
int *pi; // a ptr
int **ppi; // a two-level multilevel ptr
int ***pppi; // a three-level multilevel ptr
```

Although it's rare to encounter multilevel pointers with more than two levels, we do see pointers to pointers in two common situations. The first is when we declare an array of pointers.

```
Shape *picture[MAX]; // array of ptr to Shape
```

Because an array name decays into a pointer to its first element (see *Array Formal Arguments* [6, 17]), the name of an array of pointers is also a pointer to a pointer.

```
Shape **pic1 = picture;
```

We most often see this usage in the implementation of a class that manages a buffer of pointers:

```
template <typename T>
class PtrVector {
  public:
    explicit PtrVector( size_t capacity )
        : buf_(new T *[capacity]), cap_(capacity), size_(0) {}
    //...
  private:
    T **buf_; // ptr to array of ptr to T
    size_t cap_; // capacity
    size_t size_; // size
};
//...
PtrVector<Shape> pic2( MAX );
```

As the implementation of `PtrVector` implies, pointers to pointers can be complex and are best kept hidden.

The second common use of multilevel pointers occurs when a function needs to change the value of a pointer that is passed to it. Consider the following function that moves a pointer to refer to the next occurrence of a character in a string:

```
void scanTo( const char **p, char c ) {
    while( **p && **p != c )
        ++*p;
}
```

The first argument to `scanTo` is a pointer to the pointer whose value we want to change. That means we have to pass the address of the pointer:

```
char s[] = "Hello, World!";
const char *cp = s;
scanTo( &cp, ',' ); // move cp to first comma
```

This usage is reasonable in C, but in C++ it is more conventional, simpler, and safer to use a reference to a pointer as a function argument rather than a pointer to a pointer.

```
void scanTo( const char *&p, char c ) {
    while( *p && *p != c )
        ++p;
}
//...
char s[] = "Hello, World!";
const char *cp = s;
scanTo( cp, ',' );
```

In C++, using a reference to pointer function argument should nearly always be preferred to a pointer to pointer argument.

A common misconception is that conversions that apply to pointers also apply to pointers to pointers. This is not the case. For instance, we know that a pointer to a derived class can be converted to a pointer to its public base class:

```
Circle *c = new Circle;
Shape *s = c; // fine...
```

Because a `Circle` is-a `Shape`, it follows that a pointer to a `Circle` is also a pointer to a `Shape`. However, a pointer to a pointer to a `Circle` is not a pointer to a pointer to a `Shape`:

```
Circle **cc = &c;
Shape **ss = cc; // error!
```

The same confusion often occurs when `const` is involved. We know that it's legal to convert a pointer to non-const to a pointer to const (see *Const Pointers and Pointers to Const* [7, 21]), but we may not convert a pointer to pointer to non-const to a pointer to pointer to const:

```
char *s1 = 0;
const char *s2 = s1; // OK...
char *a[MAX]; // aka char **
const char **ps = a; // error!
```

Item 9 | New Cast Operators

There's something sneaky and underhanded about old-style casts. Their syntax is such that they can often pass unnoticed in a section of code, but they can do terrible damage, like an unexpected sucker punch from a bully. Let's clarify what we mean by "old-style" cast. Obviously, the original C syntax consisting of a parenthesized type applied to an expression is an old-style cast:

```
char *hopeItWorks = (char *)0x00ff0000; // old-style cast
```

C++ introduced another way of saying the same thing with the function-style cast syntax:

```
typedef char *PChar;
hopeItWorks =
    PChar( 0x00ff0000 ); // function-style/old-style cast
```

A function-style cast may look more civilized than its dread forebear, but it's just as nasty; avoid both of them like the plague.

Honest programmers use the new cast operators because they allow you to say more precisely what you mean, and mean more accurately what you say. There are four of them, and each has a specific purpose.

The `const_cast` operator allows you to add or remove `const` and `volatile` type qualifiers in an expression's type:

```
const Person *getEmployee() { ... }
//...
Person *anEmployee = const_cast<Person *>(getEmployee());
```

In this code, we've used `const_cast` to strip a `const` type qualifier from the return type of `getEmployee`. We could have used an old-style cast to achieve the same result,

```
anEmployee = (Person *)getEmployee();
```

but the `const_cast` is superior for a couple of reasons. First, it's obvious and hideous. It sticks out of the code like a sore thumb, and that's a good thing, because casts in any form are dangerous. They should be painful to write, because you should use them only if you have to use them. They should be easy to find, because casts are the "usual suspects" one examines first whenever a bug appears. Second, a `const_cast` is less powerful than an old-style cast because it will affect only type qualifiers. This restriction is a good thing as well, because it allows us to say more precisely what our intent is. Using an old-style cast tells the compiler to shut up because you intend that the return type of `getEmployee` be converted to `Person *`. Use of a `const_cast` tells the compiler to shut up because you intend to strip a `const` from the return type of `getEmployee`. There is not a big difference in these two statements (although they're both pretty disrespectful, really) unless some maintenance occurs to the `getEmployee` function:

```
const Employee *getEmployee(); // big change!
```

The gag rule enforced by the old-style cast is still in effect; the improper conversion of `const Employee *` to `Person *` will not be flagged by the compiler, but the compiler will complain about the `const_cast`, because that drastic a conversion is beyond its capabilities. In short, the `const_cast` is preferred to the old-style cast because it's more hideous, harder to use, and less powerful.

The `static_cast` operator is used for casts that are relatively portable across platforms. Most commonly, it is used to cast "down" an inheritance hierarchy from a base class pointer or reference toward a derived class pointer or reference (see also *Capability Queries* [27, 93]):

```
Shape *sp = new Circle;
Circle *cp = static_cast<Circle *>(sp); // downcast
```

In this case, the `static_cast` will result in correct code, because `sp` actually does refer to a `Circle` object. However, if `sp` had pointed instead to some other type of `Shape`, we would have likely gotten a runtime error of some sort when we used `cp`. To reiterate, these new cast operators are safer than old-style casts, but they're not necessarily safe.

Note that a `static_cast` may not change type qualifiers the way a `const_cast` can. This implies that it is sometimes necessary to use a sequence of two new cast operators to achieve what a single old-style cast could do:

```
const Shape *getNextShape() { ... }
//...
Circle *cp =
    static_cast<Circle *>(const_cast<Shape *>(getNextShape()));
```

The standard doesn't guarantee much about the behavior of `reinterpret_cast`, but it generally does just what its name says; it looks at the bits of an object and lets you pretend they represent something else entirely:

```
hopeItWorks = // pretend int is pointer
    reinterpret_cast<char *>(0x00ff0000);
int *hopeless = // pretend char * is int *
    reinterpret_cast<int *>(hopeItWorks);
```

This sort of thing is occasionally necessary in low-level code, but it's not likely to be portable. Proceed with caution. Note the difference between `reinterpret_cast` and `static_cast` when down casting from a pointer to a base class to a pointer to a derived class. A `reinterpret_cast` will typically just pretend the base class pointer is a derived class pointer without changing its value whereas a `static_cast` (and an old style cast, for that matter) will perform the correct address manipulation (see *Meaning of Pointer Comparison* [28, 97]).

Speaking of casting within a hierarchy brings us to `dynamic_cast`. A `dynamic_cast` is used typically to perform a safe down cast from a pointer to a base to a derived class (but see *Capability Queries* [27, 93]). The difference from `static_cast` is that a `dynamic_cast` used as a down cast may be performed only on a polymorphic type (that is, the type of the expression being cast has to be a pointer to class type with a virtual function), and the cast actually performs a runtime check to see that the cast is correct. This safety comes at a cost, though; a `static_cast` typically has no or minimal runtime cost whereas using a `dynamic_cast` implies significant runtime overhead.

```
const Circle *cp =
    dynamic_cast<const Circle *>( getNextShape() );
if( cp ) { ... }
```

If getNextShape returns a pointer to a Circle (or something publicly derived from Circle, that is, something that is-a Circle; see *Polymorphism* [2, 3]), the cast will succeed and cp will point to a Circle. Otherwise cp will be null. Note that we can combine the declaration and test in the same expression:

```
if( const Circle *cp
    = dynamic_cast<const Circle *>(getNextShape()) ) { ... }
```

This is advantageous because it restricts the scope of the variable cp to the if-statement, so cp will just go out of scope when we no longer need it.

A less common use of dynamic_cast is to perform a down cast to a reference type:

```
const Circle &rc = dynamic_cast<const Circle &>(*getNextShape());
```

The operation is similar to that of a dynamic_cast to a pointer type, but if the cast fails, the operator throws a std::bad_cast exception rather than simply returning a null pointer. (Remember, there are no null references; see *References Are Aliases, Not Pointers* [5, 13].) Idiomatically, a dynamic_cast to a pointer is asking a question ("Is this Shape pointer actually pointing to a Circle? If not, I can deal with it."), whereas a dynamic_cast to a reference is stating an invariant ("This Shape is supposed to be a Circle. If it's not, something is seriously wrong!").

As with the other new cast operators, use of dynamic_cast is occasionally necessary, but it is often overused because of its reputation for being a "safe" cast. See *Factory Method* [30, 103] for an example of such overuse.

Item 10 | Meaning of a Const Member Function

Technically, const member functions are trivial. Socially, they can be complex.

The type of the `this` pointer in a non-const member function of a class X is `X * const`. That is, it's a constant pointer to a non-constant X (see *Const Pointers and Pointers to Const* [7, 21]). Because the object to which `this` refers is not const, it can be modified. The type of `this` in a const member function of a class X is `const X * const`. That is, it's a constant pointer to a constant X. Because the object to which `this` refers is const, it cannot be modified. That's the difference between const and non-const member functions.

This is why it's possible to change the logical state of an object with a const member function even if the physical state of the object does not change. Consider the following somewhat uninspired implementation of a class X that uses a pointer to an allocated buffer to hold some portion of its state:

```
class X {
  public:
    X() : buffer_(0), isComputed_(false) {}
    //...
    void setBuffer() {
        int *tmp = new int[MAX];
        delete [] buffer_;
        buffer_ = tmp;
    }
    void modifyBuffer( int index, int value ) const // immoral!
        { buffer_[index] = value; }
    int getValue() const {
        if( !isComputed_ ) {
            computedValue_ = expensiveOperation(); // error!
```

```
            isComputed_ = true; // error!
        }
        return computedValue_;
    }
  private:
    static int expensiveOperation();
    int *buffer_;
    bool isComputed_;
    int computedValue_;
};
```

The `setBuffer` member function must be non-const because it's modifying a data member of its `X` object. However, `modifyBuffer` can legally be const because it's not changing the `X` object; it's changing only some data to which the `buffer_` member of `X` refers.

That's legal, but it's not moral. Like a shyster lawyer who follows the letter of the law while violating its intent, a C++ programmer who writes a const member function that changes the logical state of its object will be judged guilty by his or her peers, if not by the compiler. It's just wrong.

Conversely, sometimes a member function that really should be declared to be const must modify its object. This is a common situation where a value is computed by "lazy evaluation." That is, the value is not computed until the first request for it in order to speed things up in the event that the request isn't made at all. The function `X::getValue` is attempting to perform a lazy evaluation of an expensive computation, but, because it is declared to be a const member function, it is not allowed to set the values of the `isComputed_` and `computedValue_` data members of its `X` object. There is a temptation in cases like this to commit the crime of casting in order to promote the greater good of being able to declare the member function to be const:

```
int getValue() const {
    if( !isComputed_ ) {
        X *const aThis = const_cast<X *const>(this); // bad idea!
        aThis->computedValue_ = expensiveOperation();
        aThis->isComputed_ = true;
    }
    return computedValue_;
}
```

Resist the temptation. The proper way to handle this situation is to declare the relevant data members to be `mutable`:

```
class X {
  public:
    //...
    int getValue() const {
        if( !isComputed_ ) {
            computedValue_ = expensiveOperation(); // fine...
            isComputed_ = true; // also fine...
        }
        return computedValue_;
    }
  private:
    //...
    mutable bool isComputed_; // can now be modified
    mutable int computedValue_; // can now be modified
};
```

Non-static data members of a class may be declared to be `mutable`, which will allow their values to be modified by const member functions of the class (as well as by non-const member functions). This in turn allows a "logically const" member function to be declared to be const even though its implementation requires modification of its object.

The effect of const on the type of a member function's `this` pointer also explains how function overload resolution can distinguish between const and non-const versions of a member function. Consider the following omnipresent example of an overloaded index operator:

```
class X {
  public:
    //...
    int &operator [](int index);
    const int &operator [](int index) const;
    //...
};
```

Recall that the left argument of a binary overloaded member operator is passed as the `this` pointer. Therefore, in indexing an `X` object, the address of the `X` object is passed as the `this` pointer:

```
int i = 12;
X a;
a[7] = i; // this is X *const because a is non-const
const X b;
i = b[i]; // this is const X *const because b is const
```

Overload resolution will match the address of a const object with a `this` pointer that points to a const. As another example, consider the following non-member binary operator with two const arguments:

```
X operator +( const X &, const X & );
```

If we decide to declare a member analog to this overloaded operator, we should declare it to be a const member function in order to preserve the constness of the left argument:

```
class X {
  public:
    //...
    X operator +( const X &rightArg ); // left arg is non-const!
    X operator +( const X &rightArg ) const; // left arg is const
    //...
};
```

Like many areas of social life, proper programming with const in C++ is technically simple but morally challenging.

Item 11 | The Compiler Puts Stuff in Classes

C programmers are used to knowing everything there is to know about the internal structure and layout of their structs, and they have a habit of writing code that depends on a particular layout. Java programmers are used to programming in ignorance of the structural layout of their objects and sometimes assume their days of ignorance are over when they start programming in C++. In fact, safe and portable coding practices in C++ do require a certain level of healthful agnosticism about the structure and layout of class objects.

With a class, it's not always "what you see is what you get." For example, most C++ programmers know that if a class declares one or more virtual functions, then the compiler will insert in each object of that class a pointer to a virtual function table. (Actually, we are guaranteed no such thing by the standard, but that's the way all existing C++ compilers implement virtual functions.) However, C++ programmers on that dangerous verge between competence and expertise often assume that the location of the virtual function table pointer is the same from platform to platform and write code based on that assumption—a deadly error. Some compilers will place the pointer at the start of the object, some will place it at the end of the object, and, if multiple inheritance is involved, several virtual function table pointers may be scattered throughout an object. Never ass|u|me.

That's not the end of it, either. If you use virtual inheritance, your objects may keep track of the locations of their virtual base subobjects with embedded pointers, embedded offsets, or nonembedded information. You might end up with a virtual function table pointer even if your class has no virtual functions! Did I mention that the compiler is also allowed to rearrange your data members in limited ways, no matter the order in which they were declared? Is there no end to this madness?

There is. If it's important to have a class type that is guaranteed to be like a C struct, you can define a POD (standardese for "plain old data"). Certainly, built-in types such as `int`, `double`, and the like are PODs, but a C `struct` or `union`-like declaration is also a POD.

```
struct S { // a POD-struct
    int a;
    double b;
};
```

Such PODs can be as safely manipulated as the corresponding C constructs (how safe that is is as questionable in C++ as it is in C). However, if you plan to get low level with your POD, it's important that it remain a POD under maintenance, or all bets are off:

```
struct S { // no longer a POD-struct!
    int a;
    double b;
  private:
    std::string c; // some maintenance
};
```

If you're not willing to deal only with PODs, what does all this meddling by the compiler imply about how you should manipulate class objects? It implies that you should manipulate class objects at a high level rather than as collections of bits. A higher-level operation will do "the same thing" from platform to platform, but it may accomplish it differently.

For example, if you want to copy a class object, never use a block copy such as the standard `memcpy` function or the hand-coded equivalent, because that's for copying storage, not objects (*Placement New* [35, 119] discusses this difference). Rather, you should use the object's own initialization or assignment operations. An object's constructor is where the compiler sets up the hidden mechanism that implements the object's virtual functions, and the like. Simply blasting a bunch of bits into uninitialized storage may not do the right thing. Similarly, a copy of one object to another must take care not to overwrite these internal class mechanisms. For example, assignment never changes the value of an object's virtual function table pointers; they're set by the constructor and never changed for the life of the object. A bit blast may well destroy that delicate internal structure. (See also *Copy Operations* [13, 45].)

Another common problem is the assumption that a particular member of a class is resident at a given offset within an object. In particular, it's not uncommon for overly clever code to assume either that the virtual function table pointer is at offset zero (that is, it's the first thing in the class) or that the first declared data member is at offset zero. Neither of these assumptions is correct more than about half the time, and both are (of course) never correct simultaneously.

```
struct T { // not a POD
    int a_; // offset of a_ unknown
    virtual void f(); // offset of vptr unknown
};
```

I'm not going to continue in this vein, because such a list of no-no's would be long, tedious, and possibly tasteless. But the next time you find yourself making low-level assumptions about the internal structure of your classes, pause, reflect, and get your mind out of the gutter!

Item 12 Assignment and Initialization Are Different

Initialization and assignment are different operations, with different uses and different implementations.

Let's get it absolutely straight. Assignment occurs when you assign. All the other copying you run into is initialization, including initialization in a declaration, function return, argument passing, and catching exceptions.

Assignment and initialization are essentially different operations not only because they're used in different contexts but also because they do different things. This difference in operation is not so obvious in the built-in types such as `int` or `double`, because, in that case, both assignment and initialization consist simply of copying some bits (but see also *References Are Aliases, Not Pointers* [5, 13]):

```
int a = 12; // initialization, copy 0X000C to a
a = 12; // assignment, copy 0X000C to a
```

However, things can be quite different for user-defined types. Consider the following simple, nonstandard string class:

```
class String {
  public:
    String( const char *init ); // intentionally not explicit!
    ~String();
    String( const String &that );
    String &operator =( const String &that );
    String &operator =( const char *str );
    void swap( String &that );
    friend const String // concatenate
        operator +( const String &, const String & );
    friend bool operator <( const String &, const String & );
    //...
  private:
    String( const char *, const char * ); // computational
```

```
    char *s_;
};
```

Initializing a `String` object with a character string is straightforward. We allocate a buffer big enough to hold a copy of the character string and then copy.

```
String::String( const char *init ) {
    if( !init ) init = "";
    s_ = new char[ strlen(init)+1 ];
    strcpy( s_, init );
}
```

The destructor does what it does:

```
String::~String() { delete [] s_; }
```

Assignment is a somewhat more difficult job than construction:

```
String &String::operator =( const char *str ) {
    if( !str ) str = "";
    char *tmp = strcpy( new char[ strlen(str)+1 ], str );
    delete [] s_;
    s_ = tmp;
    return *this;
}
```

An assignment is somewhat like destruction followed by a construction. For a complex user-defined type, the target (left side, or `this`) must be cleaned up before it is reinitialized with the source (right side, or `str`). In the case of our `String` type, the `String`'s existing character buffer must be freed before a new character buffer is attached. See *Exception Safe Functions* [39, 135] for an explanation of the ordering of the statements. (By the way, just about every week somebody reinvents the bright idea of implementing assignment with an explicit destructor call and using placement new to call a constructor. It doesn't always work, and it's not exception safe. Don't do it.)

Because a proper assignment operation cleans up its left argument, one should never perform a user-defined assignment on uninitialized storage:

```
String *names = static_cast<String *>(::operator new( BUFSIZ ));
names[0] = "Sakamoto"; // oops! delete [] uninitialized pointer!
```

In this case, `names` refers to uninitialized storage because we called `operator new` directly, avoiding implicit initialization by `String`'s default constructor; `names` refers to a hunk of memory filled with random bits. When the `String` assignment operator is called in the second line, it will attempt to perform an array delete on an uninitialized pointer. (See *Placement New* [35, 119] for a safe way to perform an operation similar to such an assignment.)

Because a constructor has less work to do than an assignment operator (in that a constructor can assume it's working with uninitialized storage), an implementation will sometimes employ what's known as a "computational constructor" for efficiency:

```
const String operator +( const String &a, const String &b )
    { return String( a.s_, b.s_ ); }
```

The two-argument computational constructor is not intended to be part of the interface of the `String` class, so it's declared to be private.

```
String::String( const char *a, const char *b ) {
    s_ = new char[ strlen(a)+strlen(b)+1 ];
    strcat( strcpy( s_, a ), b );
}
```

Item 13 Copy Operations

Copy construction and copy assignment are different operations. Technically, they have nothing to do with each other, but socially they hang out together and must be compatible.

```
class Impl;
class Handle {
  public:
    //...
    Handle( const Handle & ); // copy constructor
    Handle &operator =( const Handle & ); // copy assignment
    void swap( Handle & );
    //...
  private:
    Impl *impl_; // pointer to implementation of Handle
};
```

Copying is such a pervasive operation that it's even more important than usual to follow convention. These operations are always declared as a pair, with the signatures above (but see *auto_ptr Is Unusual* [43, 147] and *Preventing Copying* [32, 111]). That is, for a class `X`, the copy constructor should be declared `X(const X &)`, and the copy assignment operator should be declared `X &operator =(const X &)`. It's common and often a good idea to define a member `swap` function if a member implementation of `swap` has a performance or exception safety advantage over a traditional non-member `swap`. An implementation of a typical non-member `swap` is straightforward:

```
template <typename T>
void swap( T &a, T &b ) {
    T temp(a); // T's copy ctor
    a = b; // T's copy assignment
    b = temp; // T's copy assignment
}
```

This swap (identical to the standard library swap) is defined in terms of the type T's copy operations, and it works well if T's implementation is small and simple but may be expensive otherwise. We can do better for a class such as Handle by just swapping the pointer to its implementation.

```
inline void Handle::swap( Handle &that )
    { std::swap( impl_, that.impl_ ); }
```

Remember the old comedy routine in which we're told how to get a million dollars and never pay any taxes on it? First, you get a million dollars.... In a similar vein, we can show how to write an exception safe copy assignment operation. First, you get an exception safe copy constructor and an exception safe swap operation. The rest is easy:

```
Handle &Handle::operator =( const Handle &that ) {
    Handle temp( that ); // exception safe copy construction
    swap( temp ); // exception safe swap
    return *this; // we assume temp's destruction won't throw
}
```

This technique works particularly well for "handle" classes, that is, classes that consist mostly or entirely of a pointer to their implementations. As we saw in an earlier example in this item, writing exception safe swaps for such classes is both trivial and efficient.

The subtle point of this implementation of copy assignment is that the behavior of copy construction must be compatible with that of copy assignment; they're different operations, but there is a pervasive, idiomatic assumption that they will produce indistinguishable results. That is, whether one writes

```
Handle a = ...
Handle b;
b = a; // assign a to b
```

or

```
Handle a = ...
Handle b( a ); // initialize b with a
```

the resulting value and future behavior of b should be indistinguishable whether it received that value through an assignment or an initialization.

This compatibility is particularly important when using the standard containers, because their implementations will often substitute copy construction for copy assignment, with the expectation that either operation will produce identical results (see *Placement New* [35, 119]).

A perhaps more common implementation of copy assignment has the following structure:

```
Handle &Handle::operator =( const Handle &that ) {
    if( this != &that ) {
        // do assignment...
    }
    return *this;
}
```

It's often necessary for correctness, and occasionally more efficient, to perform a check for assignment to self, that is, ensure the left side (`this`) and right side (`that`) of the assignment have different addresses.

At one time or another in their careers, most C++ programmers toy with the idea of implementing virtual copy assignment. It's legal but subtly complex, so don't do it. Clone instead (see *Virtual Constructors and Prototype* [29, 99]).

Item 14 Function Pointers

It's possible to declare a pointer to a function of a particular type.

```
void (*fp)(int); // ptr to function
```

Note the required use of parentheses to indicate that `fp` is a pointer to a function that returns `void`, not a function that returns `void *` (see *Dealing with Function and Array Declarators* [17, 61]). Like a pointer to data, a pointer to function may be null, or it may refer to a function of the appropriate type.

```
extern int f( int );
extern void g( long );
extern void h( int );
//...
fp = f; // error! &f is of type int(*)(int), not void(*)(int)
fp = g; // error! &g is of type void(*)(long), not void(*)(int)
fp = 0; // OK, set to null
fp = h; // OK, point to h
fp = &h; // OK, take address explicitly
```

Note that it is not necessary to take the address of a function explicitly when initializing or assigning its address to a pointer to function; the compiler knows implicitly to take the function's address, so using the `&` operator is optional in this case and is usually omitted.

In a similar fashion, it is not necessary to dereference a function pointer to call the function to which it refers, because the compiler will dereference it for you:

```
(*fp)(12); // explicit dereference
fp(12); // implicit dereference, same result
```

Note that no "generic" pointer exists that can point to any type of function the way a `void *` pointer can refer to any kind of data. Also note that the address of a non-static member function is not a pointer, so we can't point to a non-static member function with a function pointer (see *Pointers to Member Functions Are Not Pointers* [16, 57]).

One traditional use of function pointers is to implement callbacks (but see *Function Objects* [18, 63] and *Commands and Hollywood* [19, 67] for generally more effective callback techniques). A "callback" is a potential action that is set up in an initialization stage to be invoked in response to a future event. For example, if one were to catch on fire, it's best if one has planned out in advance how one should react:

```
extern void stopDropRoll();
inline void jumpIn() { ... }
//...
void (*fireAction)() = 0;
//...
if( !fatalist ) { // if you care that you're on fire...
    // then set an appropriate action, just in the event!
    if( nearWater )
        fireAction = jumpIn;
    else
        fireAction = stopDropRoll;
}
```

Once we've determined our course of action, a different part of our code can focus on if and when to execute the action, without being concerned with what the action is:

```
if( ftemp >= 451 ) { // if there's a fire...
    if( fireAction ) // ...and an action to execute...
        fireAction(); // ...execute it!
}
```

Note that it is legal to point to an inline function. However, calling an inline function through a function pointer will not result in an inline function call, because the compiler will not be able, in general, to determine at compile time precisely what function will be called. In our previous example, `fireAction` may point to either of two functions (or neither), so at the point of call the compiler has no choice but to generate code for an indirect, non-inline function call.

It's also legal to take the address of an overloaded function:

```
void jumpIn();
void jumpIn( bool canSwim );
//...
fireAction = jumpIn;
```

The type of the pointer is used to select among the various candidate functions. In this case, `fireAction` has type `void(*)()`, so the first `jumpIn` is selected.

Function pointers are used as callbacks in several places in the standard library, most notably by the standard `set_new_handler` function that sets a callback to be invoked if the global `operator new` function is unable to fulfill a memory request.

```
void begForgiveness() {
    logError( "Sorry!" );
    throw std::bad_alloc();
}
//...
std::new_handler oldHandler =
    std::set_new_handler(begForgiveness);
```

The standard typename `new_handler` is a typedef:

```
typedef void (*new_handler)();
```

The callback, therefore, must be a function that takes no argument and returns `void`. The `set_new_handler` function sets the callback to its argument and returns the previous callback; no separate functions exist for getting and setting. Simply getting the current callback requires some idiomatic gyrations:

```
std::new_handler current
    = std::set_new_handler( 0 ); // get...
std::set_new_handler( current ); // ...and restore!
```

The standard `set_terminate` and `set_unexpected` functions also use this combined get/set callback idiom.

Item 15 Pointers to Class Members Are Not Pointers

It's unfortunate that pointers to class members have the term "pointer" in their descriptions, because they don't contain addresses and don't behave like pointers.

The syntax for declaring a pointer to member is really not too horrible (if you're already resigned to the declarator syntax for regular pointers):

```
int *ip; // pointer to an int
int C::*pimC; // pointer to an int member of C
```

All you have to do is use `classname::*` rather than a plain `*` to indicate you're referring to a member of `classname`. Otherwise, the syntax is the same as for a regular pointer declarator.

```
void *   *    *const* weird1;
void *A::*B::*const* weird2;
```

The name `weird1` has the type pointer to const pointer to pointer to pointer to `void`. The name `weird2` has the type pointer to const pointer to a member of `B` to a pointer to a member of `A`, which is a pointer to `void`. (This is just an example, and you wouldn't normally expect to see a declaration this complex or this silly.)

A regular pointer contains an address. If you dereference a pointer, you get the object at that address:

```
int a = 12;
ip = &a;
*ip = 0;
a = *ip;
```

A pointer to member, unlike a regular pointer, does not refer to a specific memory location. Rather, it refers to a particular member of a class but not to a particular member of a particular object. Mechanically, it's usually clearest to consider a pointer to data member to be an offset. This is not necessarily the case, because the C++ standard says nothing about how a pointer to data member should be implemented; it says only what its syntax and behavior must be. However, most compilers implement pointers to data members as integers that contain the offset of the member referred to, plus one. (The offset is incremented so that the value 0 can represent a null pointer to data member.) The offset tells you how many bytes from the start of an object a particular member is located.

```
class C {
  public:
    //...
    int a_;
};
int C::*pimC; // pointer to an int member of C
C aC;
C *pC = &aC;
pimC = &C::a_;
aC.*pimC = 0;
int b = pC->*pimC;
```

When we set the value of `pimC` to `&C::a_`, we're effectively setting `pimC` with the offset of `a_` within `C`. Let's be clear: Unless `a_` is a static member, using `&` in the expression `&C::a_` does not give us an address; it gives us an offset. Note that this offset applies to any object of type `C`; that is, if the member `a_` can be found 12 bytes from the start of one `C` object, it will be found 12 bytes from the start of any other `C` object.

Given an offset of a member within a class, we need the address of an object of that class in order to get to the data member at that offset. That's where the unusual-looking `.*` and `->*` operators enter. When we write `pC->*pimC`, we are requesting that the address in `pC` be augmented by the offset in `pimC` in order to access the appropriate data member in the `C` object referred to by `pC`. When we write `aC.*pimC`, we are requesting that the address of `aC` be augmented by the offset in `pimC` in order to access the appropriate data member in the `C` object referred to by `pC`.

Pointers to data members are not as commonly used as pointers to member functions, but they are handy for illustrating the concept of contravariance.

There is a predefined conversion from a pointer to a derived class to a pointer to any of its public base classes. We often say that there is an is-a relationship from the derived class to its public base classes, and this relationship often arises naturally from an analysis of the problem domain (see *Polymorphism* [2, 3]). Therefore, we can state (for example) that a `Circle` is-a `Shape` through public inheritance, and C++ backs us up by providing an implicit conversion from `Circle *` to `Shape *`. No implicit conversion exists from a `Shape *` to a `Circle *` because such a conversion would not make sense; many different types of `Shape` may exist, and not all of them are `Circles`. (It also just sounds silly to say, "A `Shape` is a `Circle`.")

In the case of pointers to class members, the opposite situation holds: There is an implicit conversion from a pointer to a member of a base class to a pointer to a member of a publicly derived class, but there is no conversion from a pointer to a member of a derived class to a pointer to a member of any of its bases. This concept of contravariance seems counterintuitive until we remember that a pointer to data member is not a pointer to an object; it's an offset *into* an object.

```
class Shape {
    //...
    Point center_;
    //...
};
class Circle : public Shape {
    //...
    double radius_;
    //...
};
```

A `Circle` is-a `Shape`, so a `Circle` object contains a `Shape` subobject. Therefore, any offset within `Shape` is also a valid offset within `Circle`.

```
Point Circle::*loc = &Shape::center_; // OK, base to derived
```

However, a `Shape` is not (necessarily) a `Circle`, so the offset of a member of `Circle` is not (necessarily) a valid offset within a `Shape`.

```
double Shape::*extent =
    &Circle::radius_; // error! derived to base
```

It makes sense to say that a `Circle` contains all the data members of its `Shape` base class (that is, it inherits those members from `Shape`), and C++ backs us up with an implicit conversion from a pointer to member of a `Shape` to a pointer to member of a `Circle`. It doesn't make sense to say that a `Shape` contains all the data members of a `Circle` (`Shape` doesn't inherit anything from `Circle`), and C++ reminds us of that by disallowing the conversion from pointer to member of `Circle` to pointer to member of `Shape`.

Item 16 Pointers to Member Functions Are Not Pointers

When you take the address of a non-static member function, you don't get an address; you get a pointer to member function.

```
class Shape {
  public:
    //...
    void moveTo( Point newLocation );
    bool validate() const;
    virtual bool draw() const = 0;
    //...
};
class Circle : public Shape {
    //...
    bool draw() const;
    //...
};
//...
void (Shape::*mf1)( Point ) = &Shape::moveTo; // not a pointer
```

The declaration syntax of a pointer to member function is really no more difficult than that of a pointer to a regular function (which, admittedly, is bad enough as it is; see *Dealing with Function and Array Declarators* [17, 61]). As with pointers to data members, all that's necessary is to use `classname::*` rather than `*` to indicate that the function referred to is a member of `classname`. Unlike a regular pointer to function, though, a pointer to member function can refer to a const member function:

```
bool (Shape::*mf2)() const = &Shape::validate;
```

As with a pointer to data member, we need an object or pointer to an object in order to dereference a pointer to member function. In the case of a pointer to data member, we need to add the object's address to the member's offset (contained in the pointer to data member) in order to access the member. In the case of a pointer to member function, we need the object's address to use as (or to calculate; see *Meaning of Pointer Comparison* [28, 97]) the value of the `this` pointer for the function call and possibly for other reasons as well.

```
Circle circ;
Shape *pShape = &circ;
(pShape->*mf2)(); // call Shape::validate
(circ.*mf2)(); // call Shape::validate
```

The `->*` and `.*` operators must be parenthesized because they have lower precedence than the `()` operator, and we have to first find out what function to call before we call it! This is entirely analogous to the use of parentheses in an expression such as `(a+b)*c`, where we want to ensure that the lower-precedence addition is carried out before the higher-precedence multiplication.

Note that there is no such thing as a "virtual" pointer to member function. Virtualness is a property of the member function itself, not the pointer that refers to it.

```
mf2 = &Shape::draw; // draw is virtual
(pShape->*mf2)(); // call Circle::draw
```

This is one reason why a pointer to member function cannot be implemented, in general, as a simple pointer to function. The implementation of the pointer to member function must store within itself information as to whether the member function to which it refers is virtual or nonvirtual, information about where to find the appropriate virtual function table pointer (see *The Compiler Puts Stuff in Classes* [11, 37]), an offset to be added to or subtracted from the function's `this` pointer (see *Meaning of Pointer Comparison* [28, 97]), and possibly other information. A pointer to member function is commonly implemented as a small structure that contains this information, although many other implementations are also in use. Dereferencing and calling a pointer to member function usually involves examining the stored information and conditionally executing the appropriate virtual or nonvirtual function calling sequence.

As with pointers to data members, pointers to member functions exhibit contravariance: there is a predefined conversion from a pointer to a member function of a base class to a pointer to a member function of a derived class, not the reverse. This makes sense if you consider that a base class member function will attempt to access only base class members through its `this` pointer whereas a derived class function may attempt to access members that are not present in the base class.

```
class B {
  public:
    void bset( int val ) { bval_ = val; }
  private
    int bval_;
};
class D : public B {
  public:
    void dset( int val ) { dval_ = val; }
  private:
    int dval_;
};
B b;
D d;
void (B::*f1)(int) = &D::dset; // error! derived func in base ptr
(b.*f1)(12); // oops! access nonexistent dval member!
void (D::*f2)(int) = &B::bset; // OK, base func in derived ptr
(d.*f2)(11); // OK, set inherited bval data member
```

Item 17 Dealing with Function and Array Declarators

The main confusion with pointer to function and pointer to array declarations arises because the function and array modifiers have higher precedence than the pointer modifier, so parentheses are often required.

```
int *f1(); // function that returns int *
int (*fp1)(); // ptr to function that returns int
```

The same problem obtains with the high-precedence array modifier:

```
const int N = 12;
int *a1[N]; // array of N int *
int (*ap1)[N]; // ptr to array of N ints
```

Of course, once one can have a pointer to a function or to an array, one can have a pointer to such a pointer:

```
int (**ap2)[N]; // ptr to ptr to array of N ints
int *(*ap3)[N]; // ptr to array of N int *
int (**const fp2)() = 0; // const ptr to ptr to func
int *(*fp3)(); // ptr to func that returns int *
```

Note that both the argument and return types contribute to the type of a function or function pointer.

```
char *(*fp4)(int,int);
char *(*fp5)(short,short) = 0;
fp4 = fp5; // error! type mismatch
```

Things can become immeasurably more complex when function and array modifiers appear in the same declaration. Consider the following common, incorrect attempt to declare an array of function pointers:

```
int (*)()afp1[N]; // syntax error!
```

In the (erroneous) declaration above, the appearance of the function modifier `()` signaled the end of the declaration, and the appended name `afp1` signaled the start of a syntax error. It's analogous to writing an array declaration

```
int[N] a2; // syntax error!
```

that works just fine in Java but is not legal C++. The correct declaration of an array of function pointers puts the name being declared in the same location that it appears in a simple pointer to function. Then we say we want an array of those things:

```
int (*afp2[N])(); // array of N ptr to func that returns int
```

Things are starting to get unwieldy here, so it's time to reach for `typedef`.

```
typedef int (*FP)(); // ptr to func that returns int
FP afp3[N]; // array of N FP, same type as afp2
```

The use of `typedef` to simplify the syntax of complex declarations is a sign of caring for those poor maintainers who come after you. Using `typedef`, even the declaration of the standard `set_new_handler` function becomes simple:

```
typedef void (*new_handler)();
new_handler set_new_handler( new_handler );
```

So, a `new_handler` (see *Function Pointers* [14, 49]) is a pointer to a function that takes no argument and returns `void`, and `set_new_handler` is a function that takes a `new_handler` as an argument and returns a `new_handler` as a result. Simple. If you try it without `typedef`, your popularity with those who maintain your code will plummet:

```
void (*set_new_handler(void (*)()))(); // correct, but evil
```

It's also possible to declare a reference to a function.

```
int aFunc( double ); // func
int (&rFunc)(double) = aFunc; // ref to func
```

References to functions are rarely used and fill pretty much the same niche as constant pointers to functions:

```
int (*const pFunc)(double) = aFunc; // const ptr to func
```

References to arrays do provide some additional capability not provided by pointers to arrays and are discussed in *Array Formal Arguments* [6, 17].

Item 18 | Function Objects

Often you'll need something that behaves like a function pointer, but function pointers tend to be unwieldy, dangerous, and (let's admit it) passé. Often the best approach is to use a function object instead of a function pointer.

A function object, like a smart pointer (see *Smart Pointers* [42, 145]) is an ordinary class object. Whereas a smart pointer type overloads the -> and * (and possibly ->*) operators to mimic a "pointer on steroids," a function object type overloads the function call operator, `()`, to create a "function pointer on steroids." Consider the following function object that computes the next element in the well-known Fibonacci series (1, 1, 2, 3, 5, 8, 13, ...) with each call:

```
class Fib {
  public:
    Fib() : a0_(1), a1_(1) {}
    int operator ();
  private:
    int a0_, a1_;
};
int Fib::operator () {
    int temp = a0_;
    a0_ = a1_;
    a1_ = temp + a0_;
    return temp;
}
```

A function object is just a regular class object, but you can call its `operator ()` member (or members, if there is more than one) with standard function call syntax.

```
Fib fib;
//...
cout << "next two in series: " << fib()
     << ' ' << fib() << endl;
```

The syntax `fib()` is recognized by the compiler as a member function call to the `operator ()` member of `fib`, identical in meaning to `fib.operator()` but presumably easier on the eye. The advantage in this case of using a function object in preference to a function or a pointer to a function is that the state required to compute the next number in the Fibonacci series is stored within the `Fib` object itself. A function implementation would have to resort to global or local static variables or some other base trickery to retain state between invocations of the function, or the information would have to be passed to the function explicitly. Also note that unlike a function that uses static data, we can have multiple, simultaneous `Fib` objects whose calculations do not interfere with each other.

```
int fibonacci () {
    static int a0 = 0, a1 = 1; // problematic...
    int temp = a0;
    a0 = a1;
    a1 = temp + a0;
    return temp;
}
```

It's also possible and common to create the effect of a virtual function pointer by creating a function object hierarchy with a virtual `operator ()`. Consider a numeric integration facility that calculates an approximation of the area under a curve, as shown in Figure 5.

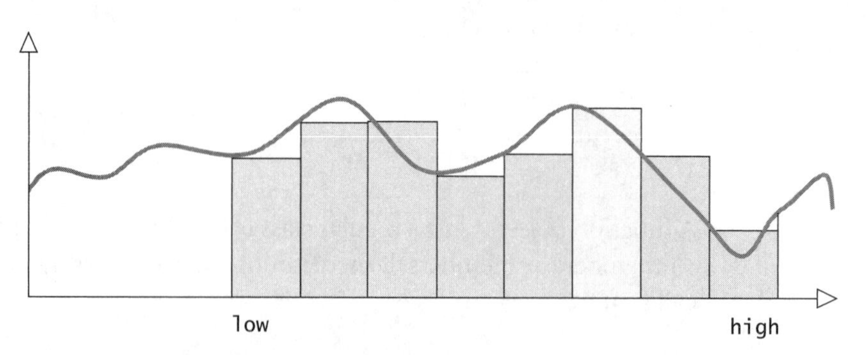

Figure 5 | Numeric integration by summing areas of rectangles (simplified)

Our integration function will iteratively call a function for values between `low` and `high` in order to approximate the area under the curve as a sum of the areas of rectangles (or some similar mechanism).

```
typedef double (*F)( double );
double integrate( F f, double low, double high ) {
    const int numSteps = 8;
    double step = (high-low)/numSteps;
    double area = 0.0;
    while( low < high ) {
        area += f( low ) * step;
        low += step;
    }
    return area;
}
```

In this version, we pass a pointer to the function over which we want to integrate.

```
double aFunc( double x ) { ... }
//...
double area = integrate( aFunc, 0.0, 2.71828 );
```

This works, but it's inflexible because it uses a function pointer to indicate the function to be integrated; it can't handle functions that require state or pointers to member functions. An alternative is to create a function object hierarchy. The base of the hierarchy is a simple interface class that declares a pure virtual `operator ()`.

```
class Func {
  public:
    virtual ~Func();
    virtual double operator ()( double ) = 0;
};
double integrate( Func &f, double low, double high );
```

Now `integrate` is capable of integrating any type of function object that is-a `Func` (see *Polymorphism* [2, 3]). It's also interesting to note that the body of `integrate` does not have to change at all (though it does require recompilation), because we use the same syntax to call a function object as we do for a pointer to function. For example, we can derive a type of `Func` that can handle non-member functions:

```
class NMFunc : public Func {
  public:
    NMFunc( double (*f)( double ) ) : f_(f) {}
    double operator ()( double d ) { return f_( d ); }
  private:
    double (*f_)( double );
};
```

This allows us to integrate all the functions of our original version:

```
double aFunc( double x ) { ... }
//...
NMFunc g( aFunc );
double area = integrate( g, 0.0, 2.71828 );
```

We can also integrate member functions by wrapping an appropriate interface around a pointer to member function and a class object (see *Pointers to Member Functions Are Not Pointers* [16, 57]):

```
template <class C>
class MFunc : public Func {
  public:
    MFunc( C &obj, double (C::*f)(double) )
        : obj_(obj), f_(f) {}
    double operator ()( double d )
        { return (obj_.*f_)( d ); }
  private:
    C &obj_;
    double (C::*f_)( double );
};
//...
AClass anObj;
MFunc<AClass> f( anObj, &AClass::aFunc );
double area = integrate( f, 0.0, 2.71828 );
```

Item 19 | Commands and Hollywood

When a function object is used as a callback, that's an instance of the Command pattern.

What's a callback? Suppose you're taking a long trip, and I lend you my car for the purpose. Given the condition of my car, I'll probably also hand you a sealed envelope with a telephone number in it, along with instructions to call the number in the envelope if you experience any engine problems. That's a callback. You do not have to know the number in advance (it may be the number of a good repair shop, a bus line, or the city dump), and in fact you may never have to call the number. In effect, the task of handling the "engine trouble" event has been partitioned between you (also known as the "framework") and me (also known as the "client of the framework"). You know when it's time to do something but not what to do. I know what to do if a particular event occurs but not when to do it. Together we make a complete application.

Callbacks are a common programming technique and have traditionally been implemented as simple pointers to functions (see *Function Pointers* [14, 49]). For example, consider an interactive button type that displays a labeled button on the screen and executes an action if it's clicked.

```
class Button {
  public:
    Button( const string &label )
        : label_(label), action_(0) {}
    void setAction( void (*newAction)() )
        { action_ = newAction; }
    void onClick() const
        { if( action_ ) action_(); }
  private:
    string label_;
    void (*action_)();
```

```
    //...
};
```

A user of a `Button` would set a callback function and then hand the `Button` over to framework code that could detect when the `Button` is clicked and execute the action.

```
extern void playMusic();
//...
Button *b = new Button( "Anoko no namaewa" );
b->setAction( playMusic );
registerButtonWithFramework( b );
```

This partitioning of responsibility is often called the "Hollywood Principle," as in "Don't call us; we'll call you." We set up the button to perform the correct action if it should ever be clicked, and the framework code knows to invoke that action if the button is clicked.

However, using a simple function pointer as a callback has severe limitations. Functions often need data with which to work, but a function pointer has no associated data. In the example above, how does the `playMusic` function know what song to play? The usual quick fix is either to severely limit the scope of the function

```
extern void playAnokoNoNamaewa();
//...
b->setAction( playAnokoNoNamaewa );
```

or to resort to disreputable and dangerous coding practices, such as the use of a global variable:

```
extern const MP3 *theCurrentSong = 0;
//...
const MP3 anokoNoNamaewa ( "AnokoNoNamaewa.mp3" );
theCurrentSong = &anokoNoNamaewa;
b->setAction( playMusic );
```

A better approach is typically to use a function object rather than a function pointer. Use of a function object—or more typically a function object hierarchy—in conjunction with the Hollywood Principle is an instance of the Command pattern.

One obvious benefit of the object-oriented approach is that a function object can have encapsulated data. Another advantage is that a function object can have dynamic behavior though virtual members; that is, we can have a hierarchy of related function objects (see *Function Objects* [18, 63]). We gain a third advantage as well, but we'll get to that later. First let's redesign our `Button` to employ the Command pattern:

```
class Action { // Command
  public:
    virtual ~Action();
    virtual void operator ()() = 0;
    virtual Action *clone() const = 0; // Prototype
};
class Button {
  public:
    Button( const std::string &label )
        : label_(label), action_(0) {}
    void setAction( const Action *newAction ) {
        Action *temp = newAction->clone();
        delete action_;
        action_ = temp;
    }
    void onClick() const
        { if( action_ ) (*action_)(); }
  private:
    std::string label_;
    Action *action_; // Command
    //...
};
```

A `Button` can now work with any function object that is-a `Action`, like this one:

```
class PlayMusic : public Action {
  public:
    PlayMusic( const string &songFile )
        : song_(songFile) {}
    void operator ()(); // plays the song
//...
  private:
    MP3 song_;
};
```

The encapsulated data (in this case, the song to play) preserves both the flexibility and safety of the `PlayMusic` function object.

```
Button *b = new Button( "Anoko no namaewa" );
auto_ptr<PlayMusic>
    song( new PlayMusic( "AnokoNoNamaewa.mp3" ) );
b->setAction( song.get() );
```

So what's the mysterious third advantage of Command to which we referred earlier? Simply that it's advantageous to work with a class hierarchy rather than a more primitive, less flexible structure like a function pointer. Because of the presence of a Command hierarchy, we've already been able to compose the Prototype pattern with Command in order to produce clonable commands (see *Virtual Constructors and Prototype* [29, 99]). We can continue in this vein and compose additional patterns with Command and Prototype for additional flexibility.

Item 20 STL Function Objects

How did we ever get by without the STL? Not only is it easier and faster to write complex code, but that code is both standard and highly optimized.

```
std::vector<std::string> names;
//...
std::sort( names.begin(), names.end() );
```

Another nice thing about the STL is that it's highly configurable. In the code above, we used `string`'s less-than operator to sort a vector of strings, but we don't always have a less-than operator to work with, or we may not want to sort in ascending order.

```
class State {
  public:
    //...
    int population() const;
    float aveTempF() const;
    //...
};
```

The `State` class (which represents a state of the union) doesn't have a less-than operator, and we probably don't want to implement one because it's not clear what it would mean for one state to be less than another (do we compare names, population, percentage of elected officials under indictment, ...?). Fortunately, the STL generally allows us to specify an alternate less-than-like operation in situations like this. Such an operation is called a "comparator," because it compares two values:

```
inline bool popLess( const State &a, const State &b )
    { return a.population() < b.population(); }
```

Once we have a comparator for `States`, we can use it to sort them:

```
State states[50];
//...
std::sort( states, states+50, popLess ); // by population
```

Here we've passed a pointer to the `popLess` function as the comparator (recall that a function name "decays" into a pointer to function when passed as an argument, just as the array name `states` decays into a pointer to its first element). Because `popLess` is passed as a function pointer, it will not be inlined in `sort`, which is unfortunate if we want a fast sort operation (see *Function Pointers* [14, 49]).

We can do better if we use a function object as a comparator:

```
struct PopLess : public std::binary_function<State,State,bool> {
    bool operator ()( const State &a, const State &b ) const
        { return popLess( a, b ); }
};
```

The `PopLess` type is a typical example of a properly constructed STL function object. First, it's a function object. It overloads the function call operator so that it may be called with the usual function call syntax. This is important, because STL generic algorithms like `sort` are written in such a way that either a function pointer or function object may be used to instantiate them, provided that they may be called with the typical function call syntax; a function object with an overloaded `operator ()` satisfies this syntactic requirement.

Second, it's derived from the standard `binary_function` base class. This is a mechanism that allows other parts of the STL implementation to ask compile-time questions of the function object (see *Embedded Type Information* [53, 189]). In this case, deriving from `binary_function` allows one to find out the argument and return types of the function object. We're not using that capability here, but you can bet that somebody else will, and we want our `PopLess` type to be used by others.

Third, the function object has no data members, no virtual functions, and no explicitly declared constructors or destructor, and the implementation of `operator ()` is inline. Function objects used as STL comparators are assumed to be small, simple, and fast. It's possible to design STL function objects with significant implementations, but it's rarely advisable. Another reason to avoid or minimize the use of data members in a function object to be used with the STL is that STL implementations may make several copies of a function object and may assume that all the copies are identical. One easy way to ensure that all copies of an object are identical is for the object to have no data at all.

Now we can sort this country out by using a function object:

```
sort( states, states+50, PopLess() );
```

Note the parentheses that follow `PopLess` in this call to `sort`. `PopLess` is a type, but we have to pass an object of that type as a function argument. By appending parentheses to the `PopLess` type name, we create an unnamed temporary `PopLess` object that exists for the duration of the function call. (These nameless objects are known as "anonymous temporaries," a term I've always enjoyed because it sounds vaguely racy.) We could have declared and passed a named object:

```
PopLess comp;
sort( states, states+50, comp );
```

However, it's more conventional, and less typing, simply to pass an anonymous temporary object.

A beneficial side effect of using a function object as our comparator is that the comparison will be inlined whereas use of a function pointer did not permit inlining. The reason the call is inlined is that the compiler knows that the type of the comparator is `PopLess` when the `sort` function template is instantiated, which in turn allows it to know that `PopLess::operator ()` will be called, which in turn allows it to inline that function, which in turn allows it to inline the nested call to `popLess`.

Another common use of a function object in the STL is as a predicate. A predicate is an operation that asks a true/false question about a single object. (You can think of a comparator as a kind of binary predicate.)

```
struct IsWarm : public std::unary_function<State,bool> {
    bool operator ()( const State &a ) const
        { return a.aveTempF() > 60; }
};
```

The design guidelines for STL predicates are identical to those for STL comparators with the exception, of course, that they're unary rather than binary functions. Starting with our previous sorted `State` results, the appropriate predicate makes it trivial to find a warm place without too many dang people:

```
State *warmandsparse = find_if( states, states+50, IsWarm() );
```

Item 21 | Overloading and Overriding Are Different

Overloading and overriding have nothing whatsoever to do with each other. Nothing. They are entirely different concepts. Ignorance of this difference, or simply sloppy use of terminology, has caused untold confusion and given rise to countless bugs.

Overloading occurs when two or more functions in the same scope have the same name and different signatures. A function's signature consists of the number and type of its declared arguments (otherwise known as "formal" arguments). When the compiler looks up a function name and finds more than one function with that name in a scope, it selects among the available candidates in that scope for the one whose formal arguments best match the actual arguments of the function call (see also *Member Function Lookup* [24, 87] and *Argument Dependent Lookup* [25, 89]). That's overloading.

Overriding occurs when a derived class function has the same name and signature as a base class virtual function. In that case, the implementation of the derived class function will replace that of the inherited base class function for virtual calls to a derived object. Overriding changes the behavior of a class but not its interface (but see *Covariant Return Types* [31, 107]).

Consider the following simple base class:

```
class B {
  public:
    //...
    virtual int f( int );
    void f( B * );
    //...
};
```

The name `f` is overloaded in `B` because two different functions named `f` are in the same scope. (The overloading is highlighted as bad code for two reasons. You probably don't want to overload a virtual function, and you probably don't want to overload on both an integral and a pointer type. See *C++ Gotchas* and *Effective C++*, respectively, to see why.)

```
class D : public B {
  public:
    int f( int );
    int f( B * );
};
```

The member function `D::f(int)` overrides the base class virtual function `B::f(int)`. The member function `D::f(B *)` doesn't override anything, because `B::f(B *)` is not virtual. It does, however, overload `D::f(int)`. Note that it does not overload the base class members `B::f`, because it's in a different scope (see also *Optional Keywords* [63, 231]).

Overloading and overriding are different concepts, and a technical understanding of their differences is essential if you want to grok advice on advanced base class interface design.

Item 22 Template Method

The Template Method pattern has nothing whatsoever to do with C++ templates. Rather, it's a way for a base class designer to give clear instructions to derived class designers concerning how the base class contract may be implemented (see *Polymorphism* [2, 3]). However, even if you think this pattern should go by a different name, please continue to use the standard name "Template Method." Much of the benefit of using patterns derives from the standard technical vocabulary they establish (see *Design Patterns* [3, 7]).

A base class specifies its contract to the world at large through its public member functions and specifies additional details for classes derived from it through its protected member functions. Private member functions may also be used as part of the implementation of a class (see *Assignment and Initialization Are Different* [12, 41]). Data members should be private, so we'll leave them out of this discussion.

The decision as to whether a base class's member function should be nonvirtual, virtual, or pure virtual is driven primarily by considering how the behavior of that function is to be customized by derived classes. After all, code that uses a base class's interface doesn't really care how a particular operation is implemented by the object; it wants to perform an operation on the object, and it's up to the object to implement that operation appropriately.

If a base class member function is nonvirtual, the base class designer is specifying an invariant over the hierarchy rooted at the base class. Derived classes should not hide a base class nonvirtual function with a derived class member of the same name (see *Member Function Lookup* [24, 87]). If you don't like the contract specified by the base class, find a different base class. Don't attempt to rewrite its contract.

Virtual and pure virtual functions specify operations whose implementations can be customized by derived classes through overriding. A non-pure virtual function provides a default implementation and does not require overriding whereas a pure virtual function must be overridden in a concrete (that is, nonabstract) derived class. Either kind of virtual function allows a derived class to plug replace its entire implementation while preserving its interface.

Use of a Template Method gives the base class designer an intermediate level of control between the "take it or leave it" nonvirtual function and the "if you don't like it, replace the whole thing" approach of a virtual function. A Template Method fixes the overall structure of its implementation but defers some portion of its implementation to derived classes. Typically, a Template Method is implemented as a public, nonvirtual function that calls protected virtual functions. The derived classes must accept the overall implementation specified in the inherited, nonvirtual base class function but may customize its behavior in limited ways by overriding the protected virtual functions it invokes.

```
class App {
  public:
    virtual ~App();
    //...
    void startup() { // Template Method
        initialize();
        if( !validate() )
            altInit();
    }
  protected:
    virtual bool validate() const = 0;
    virtual void altInit();
    //...
  private:
    void initialize();
    //...
};
```

The nonvirtual `startup` Template Method calls down to customizations provided by derived classes:

```
class MyApp : public App {
  public:
    //...
  private:
```

```
    bool validate() const;
    void altInit();
    //...
};
```

Template Method is an example of the Hollywood Principle at work; that is, "Don't call us; we'll call you" (see *Commands and Hollywood* [19, 67]). The overall flow of the `startup` function is determined by the base class, and `startup` is invoked by clients of the base class's interface, so derived class designers don't know when `validate` or `altInit` will be called. But they do know what `validate` and `altInit` should do when they are called, and together the base and derived classes cooperate to produce a complete function implementation.

Item 23 | Namespaces

Global scope was getting overly crowded. Everybody and his brother implemented libraries that reused the same names for different classes and functions. For example, many libraries wanted to include a class named `String`, but if you used two different libraries that defined a `String` type, you'd get a multiple definition error or worse. Various extra-language approaches used to address this problem (naming conventions, the preprocessor, ...) only made things worse. Namespaces to the rescue.

In some ways, namespaces introduce complexity (see *Argument Dependent Lookup* [25, 89]), but most uses of namespaces are simple and simplifying. A namespace is a subdivision of global scope:

```
namespace org_semantics {
    class String { ... };
    String operator +( const String &, const String & );
    // other classes, functions, typedefs, etc...
}
```

This code snippet opens a namespace called `org_semantics`, declares some useful things, and then closes the namespace with a closing curly brace. You can always add more to a namespace by just repeating the process; namespaces are "open."

Note that some of the names in the `org_semantics` namespace are declared but not defined. To define these names, we can reopen the namespace:

```
namespace org_semantics {
    String operator +( const String &a, String &b ) { // oops!
        //...
    }
}
```

Alternatively, we can simply qualify the definition with the namespace name without reopening the namespace:

```
org_semantics::String
org_semantics::operator +(
    const org_semantics::String &a,
    const org_semantics::String &b ) {
    //...
}
```

This has the advantage of not allowing one to inadvertently declare a new namespace name (as we did when we left out the `const` in the second argument of our first definition of `operator +`) rather than define an already declared one. Admittedly, the seemingly endless repetition of `org_semantics` in this case can be tedious, but that's the price of security! We'll discuss some approaches that can improve this situation.

If you want to use a name that's defined in a particular namespace, you have to tell the compiler in what namespace the name is to be found:

```
org_semantics::String s( "Hello, World!" );
```

Although some of the C++ standard library has remained in global scope (the standard global `operator` news, `operator deletes`, array news, and array deletes come to mind), the bulk of the standard library is now resident in the `std` (that is, "standard") namespace, and most standard library use requires qualification with the `std` namespace name:

```
#include <iostream>
#include <vector>
//...
void aFunc() {
    vector<int> a; // error! I don't see a vector!
    std::vector<int> b; // Oh, there it is!
    cout << "Oops!" << endl; // errors!
    std::cout << "Better!" << std::endl; // OK
    //...
}
```

Clearly, continual explicit qualification can be tedious. One way to relieve the tedium is to employ a "using directive."

```
void aFunc() {
    using namespace std; // using directive
```

```
    vector<int> a; // OK
    cout << "Hello!" << endl; // OK
    //...
}
```

A using directive essentially “imports” the names from the namespace, making them accessible without qualification in the scope of the using directive. In this case, the using directive is in force until the end of the function body, and then you’re back to explicit qualification. For this reason, many C++ programmers (even many who should know better) suggest putting the using directive at global scope:

```
#include <iostream>
#include <vector>
using namespace std;
using namespace org_semantics;
```

That’s a bad idea. Now we’re back nearly to square one, with all the names from a namespace available everywhere, sowing confusion and disarray. This is a particularly bad idea in a header file, where you can leverage your bad decision over any file that includes your header. In header files, we usually prefer to stick with explicit qualification and reserve using directives for smaller scopes (such as function bodies or blocks within a function) where their effects are bounded and easier to control. Basically, you have to be on your best behavior in header files and on pretty good behavior in source files, but you can kick back and relax inside a function.

One interesting aspect of using directives is that they make the names of a namespace available, but as if they were declared at global scope, not necessarily at the scope in which the using directive occurs. Local names will hide namespace names:

```
void aFunc() {
    using namespace std; // using directive
    //...
    int vector = 12; // a poorly named local variable...
    vector<int> a; // error! std::vector is hidden
    std::vector<int> b; // OK, can use explicit qualification
    //...
}
```

An alternative is a "using declaration" that provides access to a namespace name through an actual declaration:

```
void aFunc() {
    using std::vector; // using declaration
    //...
    int vector = 12; // error! redeclaration of vector
    vector<int> a; // OK
    //...
}
```

Using declarations are often a good middle ground between tedious explicit qualification and unrestrained use of using directives, particularly if a given section of code uses only a few names from two or more namespaces but uses them repeatedly:

```
void aFunc() {
    using std::cout;
    using std::endl;
    using org_semantics::String;
    String a, b, c;
    //...
    cout << a << b << c << endl;
    // etc.
}
```

Another way to deal with long, tedious namespace names is to employ an alias:

```
namespace S = org_semantics;
```

Now `S` may be used in place of `org_semantics` within the scope of the alias. Like a using directive, a namespace alias is best avoided in a header file. (`S` is likely to conflict with other names more often than `org_semantics`, after all...)

Let's finish up our quick tour of namespaces with a look at anonymous namespaces:

```
namespace {
    int anInt = 12;
    int aFunc() { return anInt; }
}
```

This anonymous namespace behaves identically to the following, where `__compiler_generated_name__` is unique for each anonymous namespace:

```
namespace __compiler_generated_name__ {
    int anInt = 12;
    int aFunc() { return anInt; }
}
using namespace __compiler_generated_name__;
```

This is the trendy new way to avoid declaring functions and variables with static linkage. In the anonymous namespace above, both `anInt` and `aFunc` have external linkage, but they can be accessed only within the translation unit (that is, preprocessed file) in which they occur, just like a static.

Item 24 Member Function Lookup

When you call a member function, there are three steps involved. First, the compiler looks up the name of the function. Second, it chooses the best matching function from the available candidates. Third, it checks that you have access to the matched function. That's it. Admittedly, each of these steps (especially the first two; see *Argument Dependent Lookup* [25, 89] and *Operator Function Lookup* [26, 91]) can be complex, but the overall function matching mechanism is as simple as one, two, three.

Most errors related to function matching stem not from misunderstanding the compiler's complex name lookup and overloaded function matching algorithms but from misunderstanding the simple, sequential nature of these three steps. Consider the following:

```
class B {
  public:
    //...
    void f( double );
};
class D : public B {
    void f( int );
};
//...
D d;
d.f( 12.3 ); // confusing
```

Which member `f` is called?

Step 1: Look up the name of the function. Because we're calling a member of a `D` object, we'll start in the scope of `D` and immediately locate `D::f`.

Step 2: Choose the best matching function from the available candidates. We have only one candidate `D::f`, so we attempt to match that one. We can do this by converting the actual argument `12.3` from `double` to `int`. (This is legal, but generally undesirable, because we'll lose precision.)

Step 3: Check access. We (may) have an error, because `D::f` is private.

The existence of a better-matching, accessible function in the base class is immaterial, because the compiler does not continue searching for a name in outer scopes once it has found one in an inner scope. An inner scope name *hides* the same name in an outer scope; it does not overload it as it does in Java.

In fact, the name does not even have to be the name of a function:

```
class E : public D {
    int f;
};
//...
E e;
e.f( 12 ); // error!
```

In this case, we have a compile-time error because our lookup of the name `f` in the scope of `E` netted us a data member, not a member function. This is, by the way, one of many reasons to establish and adhere to a simple naming convention. If the data member `E::f` had been named `f_` or `m_f`, it would not have hidden the inherited base class function `f`.

Item 25 | Argument Dependent Lookup

Namespaces have a pervasive influence on modern C++ programs and designs (see *Namespaces* [23, 81]). Some of these influences are immediately obvious, such as the presence of using declarations and directives and qualification of names with namespace scope. However, namespaces have less syntactically obvious influences that are nevertheless as basic and important. Argument dependent lookup (ADL) is one of these. Like many C++ features, ADL has the potential to be complex, but in common use it is straightforward and solves many more problems than it introduces.

The idea behind ADL is simple. When looking up the name of a function in a function call expression, the compiler will also examine namespaces that contain the types of the function call's arguments. For example, consider the following:

```
namespace org_semantics {
    class X { ... };
    void f( const X & );
    void g( X * );
    X operator +( const X &, const X & );
    class String { ... };
    std::ostream operator <<( std::ostream &, const String & );
}
//...
int g( org_semantics::X * );
void aFunc() {
    org_semantics::X a;
    f( a ); // call org_semantics::f
    g( &a ); // error! ambiguous...
    a = a + a; // call org_semantics::operator +
}
```

Ordinary lookup would not find the function org_semantics::f, because it is nested in a namespace and the use of f is not qualified with the namespace. However, the type of the argument a is defined in the org_semantics namespace, so the compiler also examines that namespace for any candidate functions.

Of course, a complex rule such as ADL can also cause some head scratching. The call to g with a pointer to an org_semantics::X is a case in point. In this case, it's possible that the coder thought the compiler would find the global g, but because the type of the actual argument was org_semantics::X *, candidate g's from that namespace were included, and the call was ambiguous. On reflection, this ambiguity is actually a good thing, because it's just as likely that the coder intended to call the function org_semantics::g rather than ::g. With the ambiguity made clear, the coder can either disambiguate the call or rename one of the functions.

Note that, even though the call to g resulted in two candidate functions for overload resolution, ::g does not overload org_semantics::g because they are not declared in the same scope (see *Overloading and Overriding Are Different* [21, 75]). ADL is a property of how a function is called, and overloading is a property of how a function is declared.

We can see the real utility of ADL with infix calls of overloaded operators, such as the use of operator + in aFunc. Here the infix expression a+a is equivalent to the call operator +(a,a), and ADL will find the overloaded operator + in the org_semantics namespace (see also *Operator Function Lookup* [26, 91]).

In fact, most C++ programmers use ADL extensively without realizing it. Consider the following common use of <iostream>:

```
org_semantics::String name( "Qwan" );
std::cout << "Hello, " << name;
```

In this case, the first (leftmost) use of operator << is most probably a call of a member function of the class template std::basic_ostream whereas the second is a non-member function call of an overloaded operator << function in the org_semantics namespace. These details are really of no interest to the author of the greeting, and ADL sorts things out rather nicely.

Item 26 Operator Function Lookup

Sometimes it looks like a member operator function overloads a non-member operator, but this is not the case. It's not overloading; it's just a different lookup algorithm. Consider the following class that overloads an operator as a member function:

```
class X {
  public:
    X operator %( const X & ) const; // binary modulus
    X memFunc1( const X & );
    void memFunc2();
    //...
};
```

We can call an overloaded operator function with either infix or function call syntax:

```
X a, b, c;
a = b % c; // infix call to member operator %
a = b.operator %( c ); // member function call
a = b.memFunc1( c ); // another member function call
```

When we use the function call syntax, the usual lookup rules apply (see *Member Function Lookup* [24, 87]), and the call `b.operator %(c)` is treated in the same way as the similar call to `memFunc1`. However, an infix call of an overloaded operator is handled differently:

```
X operator %( const X &, int ); // non-member operator
//...
void X::memFunc2() {
    *this % 12; // calls non-member operator %
    operator %( *this, 12 ); // error!  too many arguments
}
```

For an infix operator call, the compiler will consider both member and non-member functions (see also *Argument Dependent Lookup* [25, 89]), so the first, infix call to `operator %` will match the non-member. This is not an instance of overloading; it's a question of the compiler looking in two different places for candidate functions. The second, non-infix call of `operator %` follows the standard function lookup rules and finds the member function. We have an error because we are attempting to pass three arguments to a binary function. (Remember the implicit `this` argument for member functions!)

In effect, infix calls of overloaded operators implement a kind of "degenerate" ADL in which both the class of the left (or only) argument of the infix operator and the global scope are considered when determining what functions will be considered for overload resolution. ADL extends this process to include candidate operator functions in other namespaces brought in by the arguments of the operator. Note that this is not overloading. Overloading is a static property of a function declaration (see *Overloading and Overriding Are Different* [21, 75]). Both ADL and infix operator function lookup are properties of the arguments supplied to a function call.

Item 27 Capability Queries

Most times when an object shows up for work, it's capable of performing as required, because its capabilities are advertised explicitly in its interface. In these cases, we don't ask the object if it can do the job; we just tell it to get to work:

```
class Shape {
  public:
    virtual ~Shape();
    virtual void draw() const = 0;
    //...
};
//...
Shape *s = getSomeShape(); // get a shape, and tell it to...
s->draw(); // ...get to work!
```

Even though we don't know precisely what type of shape we're dealing with, we know that it is-a `Shape` and, therefore, can `draw` itself. This is a simple and efficient—and therefore desirable—state of affairs.

However, life is not always that straightforward. Sometimes an object shows up for work whose capabilities are not obvious. For example, we may have a need for a shape that can be rolled:

```
class Rollable {
  public:
    virtual ~Rollable();
    virtual void roll() = 0;
};
```

A class like `Rollable` is often called an "interface class" because it specifies an interface only, similar to a Java interface. Typically, such a class has no non-static data members, no declared constructor, a virtual destructor, and a set of pure virtual functions that specify what a `Rollable` object is capable of doing. In this case, we're saying that anything that is-a `Rollable` can `roll`. Some shapes can roll; others can't:

```
class Circle : public Shape, public Rollable { // circles roll
    //...
    void draw() const;
    void roll();
    //...
};
class Square : public Shape { // squares don't
    //...
    void draw() const;
    //...
};
```

Of course, other types of objects in addition to shapes may be rollable:

```
class Wheel : public Rollable { ... };
```

Ideally, our code should be partitioned in such a way that we always know whether we are dealing with objects that are `Rollable` before we attempt to `roll` them, just as we earlier knew we were dealing with `Shapes` before we attempted to `draw` them.

```
vector<Rollable *> rollingStock;
//...
for( vector<Rollable *>::iterator i( rollingstock.begin() );
                                i != rollingStock.end(); ++i )
    (*i)->roll();
```

Unfortunately, we occasionally run up against situations where we simply do not know if an object has a required capability. In such cases, we are forced to perform a capability query. In C++, a capability query is typically expressed as a `dynamic_cast` between unrelated types (see *New Cast Operators* [9, 29]).

```
Shape *s = getSomeShape();
Rollable *roller = dynamic_cast<Rollable *>(s);
```

This use of `dynamic_cast` is often called a "cross-cast," because it attempts a conversion across a hierarchy, rather than up or down a hierarchy, as shown in Figure 6.

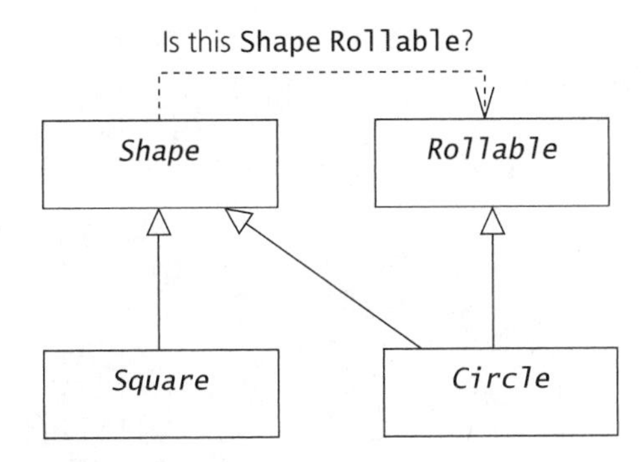

Figure 6 A capability query: "May I tell this shape to roll?"

If `s` refers to a `Square`, the `dynamic_cast` will fail (result in a null pointer), letting us know that the `Shape` to which `s` refers is not also `Rollable`. If `s` refers to a `Circle` or to some other type of `Shape` that is also derived from `Rollable`, then the cast will succeed, and we'll know that we can `roll` the shape.

```
Shape *s = getSomeShape();
if( Rollable *roller = dynamic_cast<Rollable *>(s) )
    roller->roll();
```

Capability queries are occasionally required, but they tend to be overused. They are often an indicator of bad design, and it's best to avoid making runtime queries about an object's capabilities unless no other reasonable approach is available.

Item 28 | Meaning of Pointer Comparison

In C++, an object can have multiple, valid addresses, and pointer comparison is not a question about addresses. It's a question about object identity.

```
class Shape { ... };
class Subject { ... };
class ObservedBlob : public Shape, public Subject { ... };
```

In this hierarchy, `ObservedBlob` is derived from both `Shape` and `Subject`, and (because the derivation is public) there are predefined conversions from an `ObservedBlob` to either of its base classes.

```
ObservedBlob *ob = new ObservedBlob;
Shape *s = ob; // predefined conversion
Subject *subj = ob; // predefined conversion
```

The availability of these conversions means that a pointer to an `ObservedBlob` may be compared to a pointer to either of its base classes.

```
if( ob == s ) ...
if( subj == ob ) ...
```

In this case, both of these conditions will be true even if the addresses contained in `ob`, `s`, and `subj` differ. Consider two possible memory layouts for the `ObservedBlob` object to which these pointers refer, as shown in Figure 7.

Under layout #1, `s` and `subj` refer to `Shape` and `Subject` subobjects within the complete object that have different addresses from the complete object to which `ob` refers. Under layout #2, the `Shape` subobject happens to have the same address as the `ObservedBlob` complete object, so `ob` and `s` contain the same address.

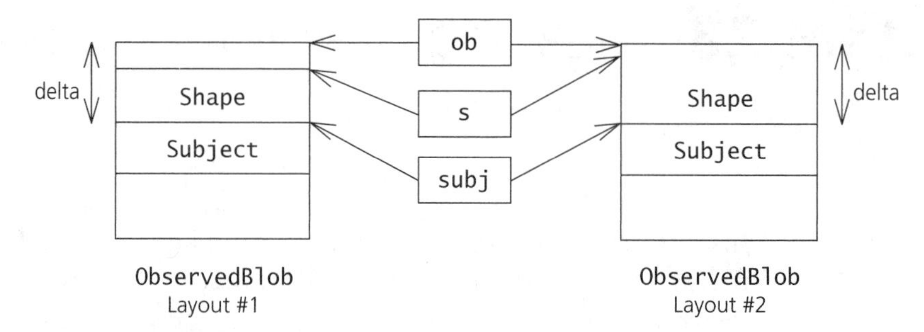

Figure 7 | Two possible layouts for an object under multiple inheritance. Under either layout, the object has multiple addresses.

Under either layout, `ob`, `s`, and `subj` refer to the same `ObservedBlob` object, so the compiler must ensure that `ob` compares equal to both `s` and `subj`. (We can't compare `s` with `subj` because they have no inheritance relationship.) The compiler accomplishes this comparison by adjusting the value of one of the pointers being compared by the appropriate offset. For example, the expression

```
ob == subj
```

may be (loosely) translated as

```
ob ? (ob+delta == subj) : (subj == 0)
```

where `delta` is the offset of the `Subject` subobject in an `ObservedBlob`. In other words, `ob` and `subj` are equal if they're both null; otherwise, `ob` is adjusted to refer to its `Subject` base class subobject and then compared to `subj`.

One important lesson to be drawn from these observations is that we must be careful to avoid losing type information when dealing with pointers and references to objects (and in general). Pointers to `void` are common culprits:

```
void *v = subj;
if( ob == v ) // not equal!
```

Once we've stripped the address contained in `subj` of its type information by copying it to a `void *`, the compiler has no choice but to fall back on raw address comparison, and with pointers to class objects that's rarely appropriate.

Item 29 | Virtual Constructors and Prototype

Suppose you find yourself in a Swedish restaurant, and you'd like to order a meal. Unfortunately, your knowledge of Swedish is limited to technical correspondence, cursing, or (typically) a combination of the two. The menu is in Swedish, and you can't read Swedish, but you do notice a gentleman on the other side of the room who is really enjoying his meal. Therefore, you call over the waiter and say

> *If that gentleman is having fish, I'd like fish. If he's having spaghetti, I'd like spaghetti too. Otherwise, if he's having eel, then eel it is. However, if he has decided on the preserved kumquats, then I'll have those.*

Does this sound reasonable? Of course not. (For one thing, you probably don't want to order spaghetti in a Swedish restaurant.) This procedure has two basic problems. First, it's tedious and inefficient. Second, it can fail. What would happen if you come to the end of your sequence of questions and you still haven't been able to guess what the other diner is eating? The waiter will walk off, leaving you stranded and hungry. Even if you happen to know the entire content of the menu and are therefore guaranteed of (eventual) success, your list of questions may become invalid or incomplete if the menu is modified between your visits to the restaurant.

The proper approach, of course, is simply to call the waiter over and say, "I'd like what that gentleman is having."

If the waiter is a literalist, he'll snatch up the other diner's half-finished meal and bring it to your table. However, that sort of behavior can lead to hurt feelings and even a food fight. This is the sort of unpleasantness that can occur when two diners try to consume the same meal at the same time. If he knows his business, the waiter will deliver an exact copy of the other diner's meal to you, without affecting the state of the meal that is copied.

These are the two major reasons for cloning: You must (or you prefer to) remain in ignorance about the precise type of object you're dealing with, and you don't want to effect change or be affected by changes to the original object.

A member function that provides the ability to clone an object is traditionally called a "virtual constructor" in C++. Of course, there are no virtual constructors, but producing a copy of an object generally involves indirect invocation of its class's copy constructor through a virtual function, giving the effect—if not the reality—of virtual construction. More recently, this technique has been called an instance of the Prototype pattern.

Of course, we have to know *something* about the object to which we refer. In our case, we know that what we want is-a meal.

```
class Meal {
  public:
    virtual ~Meal();
    virtual void eat() = 0;
    virtual Meal *clone() const = 0;
    //...
};
```

The `Meal` type provides the ability to clone with the `clone` member function. The `clone` function is actually a specialized kind of Factory Method (see *Factory Method* [30, 103]) that manufactures an appropriate product while allowing the invoking code to remain in ignorance of the exact type of context and product class. Concrete classes derived from `Meal` (that is, those meals that actually exist and are listed on the menu) must provide an implementation of the pure virtual `clone` operation.

```
class Spaghetti : public Meal {
  public:
    Spaghetti( const Spaghetti & ); // copy ctor
    void eat();
    Spaghetti *clone() const
        { return new Spaghetti( *this ); } // call copy ctor
    //...
};
```

(For an explanation as to why the return type of the overriding derived class `clone` function differs from that of the base class function, see *Covariant Return Types* [31, 107].)

With this simple framework in place, we have the ability to produce a copy of any type of `Meal` without precise knowledge about the actual type of the `Meal` we're copying. Note that the following code has no mention of concrete derived classes and therefore no coupling of the code to any current *or future* types derived from `Meal`.

```
const Meal *m = thatGuysMeal(); // whatever he's having...
Meal *myMeal = m->clone(); // ...I want one too!
```

In fact, we could end up ordering something we've never even heard of. In effect, with Prototype, ignorance of the existence of a type is no barrier to creating an object of that type. The polymorphic code above can be compiled and distributed, and later augmented with new types of `Meal` without the need for recompilation.

This example illustrates some of the advantages of ignorance in software design, particularly in the design of software structured as a framework that is designed for customization and extension: The less you know, the better.

Item 30 | Factory Method

A high-level design often requires the creation of an object of the "appropriate" type, based on the type of an existing object. For example, we may have a pointer or reference to an `Employee` object of some kind, and we need to generate the appropriate kind of `HRInfo` object for that type of `Employee`, as shown in Figure 8.

Here we have almost parallel `Employee` and `HRInfo` hierarchies. `Salary` and `Hourly` employees require the generation of an `StdInfo` object whereas a `Temp` requires a `TempInfo` object.

The high-level design is simple: "Create the appropriate type of record for this employee." Unfortunately, programmers often see such a requirement as an excuse to engage in runtime type queries. That is, the code that implements this requirement simply asks a series of questions about the exact type of `Employee` in order to determine the type of `HRInfo` object to generate.

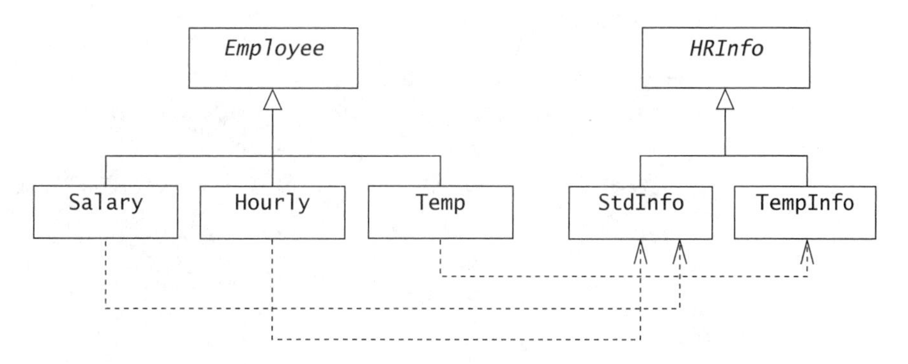

Figure 8 | Pseudoparallel hierarchies. How should we map an employee to its corresponding human resources information?

One common approach that is always wrong is to use a type code and a switch-statement:

```
class Employee {
  public:
    enum Type { SALARY, HOURLY, TEMP };
    Type type() const { return type_; }
    //...
  private:
    Type type_;
    //...
};
//...
HRInfo *genInfo( const Employee &e ) {
    switch( e.type() ) {
    case SALARY:
    case HOURLY: return new StdInfo( e );
    case TEMP:return new TempInfo( static_cast<const Temp*>(e) );
    default: return 0; // unknown type code!
    }
}
```

Nearly as bad is the use of `dynamic_cast` to ask a series of personal questions of the `Employee` object:

```
HRInfo *genInfo( const Employee &e ) {
    if( const Salary *s = dynamic_cast<const Salary *>(&e) )
        return new StdInfo( s );
    else if( const Hourly *h = dynamic_cast<const Hourly *>(&e) )
        return new StdInfo( h );
    else if( const Temp *t = dynamic_cast<const Temp *>(&e) )
        return new TempInfo( t );
    else
        return 0; // unknown employee type!
}
```

The major flaw with both of these implementations of `genInfo` is that they are coupled to all the concrete types derived from both `Employee` and `HRInfo`, and they must be familiar with the mapping from each employee type to its appropriate HRInfo type. Any change in the set of Employees, in the set of HRInfos, or in the mapping from one to the other requires maintenance of the code. In the likely event that different groups will be adding (and removing) new types from these hierarchies on a continuing basis, it's unlikely that this maintenance will always be correctly performed. Another problem is that either approach can fail to identify the exact type of the Employee argument, which will require the code that calls genInfo to make provision to handle the error.

The correct approach is to consider where the mapping from each Employee type to the appropriate HRInfo type should reside. Put another way, who knows best what type of HRInfo object a Temp employee requires? The Temp employee itself, of course:

```
class Temp : public Employee {
  public:
    //...
    TempInfo *genInfo() const
        { return new TempInfo( *this ); }
    //...
};
```

We still have a problem in that we may not know that we are dealing with a Temp employee rather than some other type of employee. But that's easy to fix with a virtual function:

```
class Employee {
  public:
    //...
    virtual HRInfo *genInfo() const = 0; // Factory Method
    //...
};
```

This is an instance of the Factory Method pattern. Rather than ask a series of blunt personal questions of an employee, we are, in effect, saying, "Whatever type of employee you are, generate the appropriate type of information for yourself."

```
Employee *e = getAnEmployee();
//...
HRInfo *info = e->genInfo(); // use Factory Method
```

The essence of Factory Method is that the base class provides a virtual function hook for generating an appropriate "product." Each derived class may override that inherited virtual function to generate an appropriate product for itself. In effect, we have the ability to use an object of unknown type ("some type of employee") to generate an object of unknown type ("the appropriate type of information").

Use of a Factory Method is often indicated when a high-level design requires generation of the "appropriate" object based on the exact type of another object, in the case of parallel or almost parallel hierarchies, and is often the cure for a series of runtime type queries.

Item 31 Covariant Return Types

Generally, an overriding function must have the same return type as the function it overrides:

```
class Shape {
  public:
    //...
    virtual double area() const = 0;
    //...
};
class Circle : public Shape {
  public:
    float area() const; // error! different return type
    //...
};
```

However, this rule is relaxed for what are known as "covariant return types." If `B` is a class type, and a base class virtual function returns `B *`, then an overriding derived class function may return `D *`, where `D` is publicly derived from `B`. (That is, `D` is-a `B`.) If a base class virtual function returns `B &`, then an overriding derived class function may return `D &`. Consider the following clone operation on a shape hierarchy (see *Virtual Constructors and Prototype* [29, 99]):

```
class Shape {
  public:
    //...
    virtual Shape *clone() const = 0; // Prototype
    //...
};
class Circle : public Shape {
  public:
    Circle *clone() const;
    //...
};
```

The overriding derived class function is declared to return a `Circle *` rather than a `Shape *`. This is legal because `Circle` is-a `Shape`. Note that the `Circle *` return value from `Circle::clone` is automatically converted to `Shape *` if the `Circle` is being manipulated as a `Shape` (see *Meaning of Pointer Comparison* [28, 97]):

```
Shape *s1 = getACircleOrOtherShape();
Shape *s2 = s1->clone();
```

The advantage of using covariant return types comes when manipulating derived types directly, rather than through their base class interfaces:

```
Circle *c1 = getACircle();
Circle *c2 = c1->clone();
```

Without a covariant return, `Circle::clone` would have to match exactly the return type of `Shape::clone` and return a `Shape *`. We'd be forced to cast the return result to `Circle *`.

```
Circle *c1 = getACircle();
Circle *c2 = static_cast<Circle *>(c1->clone());
```

As another example, consider the following Factory Method member of `Shape` that returns a reference to an appropriate shape editor for the concrete shape (see *Factory Method* [30, 103]):

```
class ShapeEditor { ... };
class Shape {
  public:
    //...
    virtual const ShapeEditor &
        getEditor() const = 0; // Factory Method
    //...
};
//...
class Circle;
class CircleEditor : public ShapeEditor { ... };
class Circle : public Shape {
  public:
    const CircleEditor &getEditor() const;
    //...
};
```

In this case, note that `CircleEditor` had to be completely defined (not simply declared) prior to the declaration of `Circle::getEditor`. The compiler has to know the layout of the `CircleEditor` object so it can perform the appropriate address manipulations to convert a `CircleEditor` reference (or pointer) into a `ShapeEditor` reference (or pointer). See *Meaning of Pointer Comparison* [28, 97].

The advantage of the covariant return is that we can always work at the appropriate level of abstraction. If we're working with `Shapes`, we'll get an abstract `ShapeEditor`; if we're working with a specific type of shape, such as `Circle`, we'll be able to deal directly with `CircleEditors`. The covariant return relieves us from having to use an error-prone cast to resupply type information that we should not have lost in the first place:

```
Shape *s = getACircleOrOtherShape();
const ShapeEditor &sed = s->getEditor();
Circle *c = getACircle();
const CircleEditor &ced = c->getEditor();
```

Item 32 | Preventing Copying

Access specifiers (`public`, `protected`, and `private`) can be used to express and enforce higher-level constraints on how a type may be used.

The most common of these techniques is to disallow copying of an object by declaring its copy operations to be private and not defining them:

```
class NoCopy {
  public:
    NoCopy( int );
    //...
  private:
    NoCopy( const NoCopy & ); // copy ctor
    NoCopy &operator =( const NoCopy & ); // copy assignment
};
```

It's necessary to declare the copy constructor and copy assignment operator, since otherwise the compiler would declare them implicitly, as public inline members. By declaring them to be private, we forestall the compiler's meddling and ensure that any use of the operations—whether explicit or implicit—will result in a compile-time error:

```
void aFunc( NoCopy );
void anotherFunc( const NoCopy & );
NoCopy a( 12 );
NoCopy b( a ); // error! copy ctor
NoCopy c = 12; // error! implicit copy ctor
a = b; // error! copy assignment
aFunc( a ); // error! pass by value with copy ctor
aFunc( 12 ); // error! implicit copy ctor
anotherFunc( a ); // OK, pass by reference
anotherFunc( 12 ); // OK
```

Item 33 | Manufacturing Abstract Bases

Abstract base classes typically represent abstract concepts from the problem domain, and therefore it doesn't make sense to declare objects of those types. We make a base class abstract by declaring (or inheriting) at least one pure virtual function, and the compiler will then ensure that no objects of the abstract base class can be created.

```
class ABC {
  public:
    virtual ~ABC();
    virtual void anOperation() = 0; // pure
    //...
};
```

However, there may be cases where we have no reasonable candidate for a pure virtual function but still want the class to act like an abstract base. In those cases, we can approximate the nature of an abstract class by making sure that there are no public constructors in the class. This invariably means we must explicitly declare at least one constructor, since otherwise the compiler will implicitly declare a public inline default constructor. Since the compiler will also declare an implicit copy constructor if we don't declare one explicitly, we typically must declare two constructors.

```
class ABC {
  public:
    virtual ~ABC();
  protected:
    ABC();
    ABC( const ABC & );
    //...
};
class D : public ABC {
    //...
};
```

The constructors are declared protected to allow their use by derived class constructors, while preventing the creation of standalone ABC objects.

```
void func1( ABC );
void func2( ABC & );
ABC a; // error! protected default ctor
D d; // OK
func1( d ); // error! protected copy ctor
func2( d ); // OK, no copy ctor
```

Another way to coerce a class into being an abstract base class is to bite the bullet and designate one of its virtual functions as pure. Often the destructor is a good choice:

```
class ABC {
  public:
    virtual ~ABC() = 0;
    //...
};
//...
ABC::~ABC() { ... }
```

Note that it is necessary, in this case, to provide an implementation of the pure virtual function since derived class destructors will call their base class destructors implicitly. (Note that this implicit call to a base class destructor from within a derived class destructor is always a non-virtual call.)

A third approach applies when a class has no virtual functions at all and no need for explicitly declared constructors. In this case, a protected, non-virtual destructor is a good approach.

```
class ABC {
  protected:
    ~ABC();
  public:
    //...
};
```

A protected destructor has basically the same effect as a protected constructor, but the error occurs when the object goes out of scope or is explicitly destroyed rather than when it is created:

```
void someFunc() {
    ABC a; // no error yet...
    ABC *p = new ABC; // no error yet...
    //...
    delete p; // error! protected dtor
    // error! implicit call to a's dtor
}
```

Item 34 | Restricting Heap Allocation

Sometimes it's a good idea to indicate that objects of a particular class should not be allocated on the heap. Often this is to ensure that the object's destructor is called, as in the case of a "handle" object that maintains a reference count for a "body" object. Local objects with automatic storage class will have their destructors called automatically (except in the case of abnormal program termination via an `exit` or `abort`), as will objects with static storage class (except in the case of an `abort`), whereas heap-allocated objects must be destroyed explicitly.

One way to indicate such a preference is by defining heap memory allocation to be illegal:

```
class NoHeap {
  public:
    //...
  protected:
    void *operator new( size_t ) { return 0; }
    void operator delete( void * ) {}
};
```

Any conventional attempt to allocate a `NoHeap` object on the heap will result in a compile-time error (see *Class-Specific Memory Mangement* [36, 123]):

```
NoHeap *nh = new NoHeap; // error! protected NoHeap::operator new
//...
delete nh; // error! protected NoHeap::operator delete
```

The `operator new` and `operator delete` members are defined (as well as declared) because they may be called implicitly from constructors and destructors on some platforms. They are declared to be protected for the same reason; they may be invoked implicitly from derived class constructors and destructors. If NoHeap is not intended for use as a base class, these functions may be declared to be private.

At the same time, we may also want to pay attention to allocation of arrays of NoHeap objects (see *Array Allocation* [37, 127]). In this case, we can simply declare array new and array delete to be private and undefined, similar to the way we deny copy operations (see *Preventing Copying* [32, 111]).

```
class NoHeap {
  public:
    //...
  protected:
    void *operator new( size_t ) { return 0; }
    void operator delete( void * ) {}
  private:
    void *operator new[]( size_t );
    void operator delete[]( void * );
};
```

It's also possible to encourage, rather than discourage, heap allocation. Just make the destructor private:

```
class OnHeap {
    ~OnHeap();
  public:
    void destroy()
        { delete this; }
    //...
};
```

Any ordinary attempt to declare an automatic or static OnHeap object will result in an implicit destructor call when the object's name goes out of scope.

```
OnHeap oh1; // error! implicit call of private dtor
void aFunc() {
    OnHeap oh2;
    //...
    // error! implicit dtor call for oh2
}
```

Item 35 | Placement New

It's impossible to call a constructor directly. However, we can trick the compiler into calling a constructor for us through the use of placement new.

```
void *operator new( size_t, void *p ) throw()
    { return p; }
```

Placement new is a standard, global, overloaded version of `operator new` that cannot be replaced with a user-defined version (unlike the standard, global, "usual" `operator new` and `operator delete` that can be replaced but probably shouldn't be). The implementation ignores the size argument and returns its second argument. This has the effect of allowing one to "place" an object at a particular location, giving the effect of being able to call a constructor.

```
class SPort { ... }; // represents a serial port
const int comLoc = 0x00400000; // location of a port
//...
void *comAddr = reinterpret_cast<void *>(comLoc);
SPort *com1 = new (comAddr) SPort; // create object at comLoc
```

It's important to distinguish the `new` operator from functions that are named `operator new`. The `new` operator can't be overloaded and so always behaves in the same way; it calls a function named `operator new` and then initializes the returned storage. Any variation of behavior we achieve with memory allocation has to do with different, overloaded versions of `operator new`, not with the `new` operator. The same applies to the `delete` operator and `operator delete`.

Placement new is a version of the function `operator new` that doesn't actually allocate any storage; it just returns a pointer to some storage that (presumably) is already allocated. Because no storage is allocated by a call to placement new, it's important not to delete it.

```
delete com1; // oops!
```

However, even though we didn't allocate any storage, we did create an object, and that object should be destroyed at the end of its lifetime. We avoid the `delete` operator and instead call the object's destructor directly:

```
com1->~SPort(); // call dtor but not operator delete
```

Designs that involve direct destructor invocation tend to be prone to error, however, often resulting in multiple destruction of the same object or no destruction of an object. We would typically prefer to employ such designs only when necessary, in well-hidden and well-maintained areas of our code.

We also have a placement array new that can be used to create an array of objects at a given location:

```
const int numComs = 4;
//...
SPort *comPorts = new (comAddr) SPort[numComs]; // create array
```

Of course, these array elements must eventually be destroyed:

```
int i = numComs;
while( i )
    comPorts[--i].~SPort();
```

One potential problem with arrays of class objects is that each element must be initialized by a call to a default constructor when the array is allocated. Consider a simple, fixed-size buffer to which one can append a new value:

```
string *sbuf = new string[BUFSIZ]; // BUFSIZ default ctor calls!
int size = 0;
void append( string buf[], int &size, const string &val )
    { buf[size++] = val; } // wipe out default initialization!
```

If only a portion of the array is used, or if the elements are immediately assigned, this is inefficient. Worse, if the element type of the array has no default constructor, we'll get a compile-time error.

Placement new is often used to address this buffer problem. With this approach the storage for the buffer is allocated in such a way as to avoid initialization by the default constructor (if any).

```
const size_t n = sizeof(string) * BUFSIZE;
string *sbuf = static_cast<string *>(::operator new( n ));
int size = 0;
```

We can't assign to an array element on its first access because it hasn't been initialized (see *Assignment and Initialization Are Different* [12, 41]). Instead, we use placement new to initialize the element with the copy constructor:

```
void append( string buf[], int &size, const string &val )
    { new (&buf[size++]) string( val ); } // placement new
```

As usual, with placement new we are required to do our own cleanup:

```
void cleanupBuf( string buf[], int size ) {
    while( size )
        buf[--size].~string(); // destroy initialized elements
    ::operator delete( buf ); // free storage
}
```

This approach is fast, clever, and not intended for viewing by the general public. This basic technique is used extensively (in a more sophisticated form) in most implementations of the standard library containers.

Item 36 Class-Specific Memory Management

If you don't like the way standard `operator new` and `operator delete` are treating one of your class types, you don't have to stand for it. Instead, your types can have their own `operator new` and `operator delete` customized to their needs.

Note that we can't do anything with the `new` operator or the `delete` operator, since their behavior is fixed, but we can change which `operator new` and `operator delete` they invoke (see *Placement New* [35, 119]). The best way to do this is to declare member `operator new` and `operator delete` functions:

```
class Handle {
  public:
    //...
    void *operator new( size_t );
    void operator delete( void * );
    //...
};
//...
Handle *h = new Handle; // uses Handle::operator new
//...
delete h; // uses Handle::operator delete
```

When we allocate an object of type `Handle` in a new expression, the compiler will first look in the scope of `Handle` for an `operator new`. If it doesn't find one, then it will use an `operator new` from the global scope. A similar situation holds for `operator delete`, so it generally makes sense to define a member `operator delete` if you define a member `operator new`, and vice versa.

Member `operator new` and `operator delete` are static member functions (see *Optional Keywords* [63, 231]), which makes sense. Recall that static member functions have no `this` pointer, and these functions are charged with simply getting and releasing the storage for an object, so they have no use for a `this` pointer. Like other static member functions, they are inherited by derived classes:

```
class MyHandle : public Handle {
    //...
};
//...
MyHandle *mh = new MyHandle; // uses Handle::operator new
//...
delete mh; // uses Handle::operator delete
```

Of course, if `MyHandle` had declared its own `operator new` and `operator delete`, those would have been found first by the compiler during lookup, and they would have been used instead of the inherited versions from the `Handle` base class.

If you define member `operator new` and `operator delete` in a base class, ensure that the base class destructor is virtual:

```
class Handle {
  public:
    //...
    virtual ~Handle();
    void *operator new( size_t );
    void operator delete( void * );
    //...
};
class MyHandle : public Handle {
    //...
    void *operator new( size_t );
    void operator delete( void *, size_t ); // note 2nd arg
    //...
};
//...
Handle *h = new MyHandle; // uses MyHandle::operator new
//...
delete h; // uses MyHandle::operator delete
```

Without a virtual destructor, the effect of deleting a derived class object through a base class pointer is undefined! The implementation may simply (and probably incorrectly) invoke `Handle::operator delete` rather than `MyHandle::operator delete`, but anything at all could happen. Notice also that we've employed a two-argument version of `operator delete` rather than the usual one-argument version. This two-argument version is another "usual" version of member `operator delete` often employed by base classes that expect derived classes to inherit their `operator delete` implementation. The second argument will contain the size of the object being deleted—information that is often useful in implementing custom memory management.

A common misconception is that use of the `new` and `delete` operators implies use of the heap (or freestore) memory, but this is not the case. The only implication in using the `new` operator is that a function called `operator new` will be called and that function will return a pointer to some memory. The standard, global `operator new` and `operator delete` do indeed allocate memory from the heap, but member `operator new` and `operator delete` can do whatever they like. There is no restriction as to where that memory comes from; it may come from a special heap, from a statically allocated block, from the guts of a standard container, or from a block of storage local to a function. The only limit to where the memory comes from is your creativity and common sense. For example, `Handle` objects could be allocated from a static block like this:

```
struct rep {
    enum { max = 1000 };
    static rep *free; // head of freelist
    static int num_used; // number of slots used
    union {
        char store[sizeof(Handle)];
        rep *next;
    };
};
static rep mem[ rep::max ]; // block of static storage
void *Handle::operator new( size_t ) {
    if( rep::free ) { // if something on freelist
        rep *tmp = rep::free; // take from freelist
        rep::free = rep::free->next;
        return tmp;
```

```
    }
    else if( rep::num_used < rep::max ) // if slots left
        return &mem[ rep::num_used++ ]; // return unused slot
    else // otherwise, we're...
        throw std::bad_alloc(); // ...out of memory!
}
void Handle::operator delete( void *p ) { // add to freelist
    static_cast<rep *>(p)->next = rep::free;
    rep::free = static_cast<rep *>(p);
}
```

A production-quality version of this implementation would take care to be more robust in out-of-memory conditions, deal with types derived from `Handle` and arrays of `Handles`, and so on, but this simple code nevertheless shows that `new` and `delete` don't necessarily have to deal with heap memory.

Item 37 Array Allocation

Most C++ programmers know to keep the array and nonarray forms straight when allocating and deallocating memory.

```
T *aT = new T; // non-array
T *aryT = new T[12]; // array
delete [] aryT; // array
delete aT; // non-array
aT = new T[1]; // array
delete aT; // error! should be array
```

The reason it's important to keep these functions properly paired is that array allocation and deallocation use different functions from nonarray allocation and deallocation. A new expression does not use `operator new` to allocate storage for an array. It uses array new. Similarly, a delete expression does not invoke `operator delete` to free an array's storage; it invokes array delete. To be precise, when you allocate an array, you're using a different operator (`new[]`) than you do when you allocate a nonarray (`new`), and likewise for deallocation.

Array new and array delete are array analogs of `operator new` and `operator delete` and are declared similarly:

```
void *operator new( size_t ) throw( bad_alloc ); // operator new
void *operator new[]( size_t ) throw( bad_alloc ); // array new
void operator delete( void * ) throw(); // operator delete
void operator delete[]( void * ) throw(); // array delete
```

The most common source of confusion with the array forms of these functions occurs when a particular class or hierarchy defines its own memory management with member `operator new` and `operator delete` (see *Class-Specific Memory Management* [36, 123]).

```
class Handle {
  public:
    //...
```

```
    void *operator new( size_t );
    void operator delete( void * );
    //...
};
```

The `Handle` class has defined nonarray memory management functions, but these won't be called for an array of `Handle`s; the global array new and array delete will:

```
Handle *handleSet = new Handle[MAX]; // calls ::operator new[]
//...
delete [] handleSet; // calls ::operator delete[]
```

Logically, it would seem to be a good idea always to declare the array forms of these functions whenever the nonarray forms exist (though, strangely, it doesn't appear to be a common practice). If the intent is really to invoke the global array allocation operations, it's clearer if the local forms just forward the call:

```
class Handle {
  public:
    //...
    void *operator new( size_t );
    void operator delete( void * );
    void *operator new[]( size_t n )
        { return ::operator new( n ); }
    void operator delete[]( void *p )
        { ::operator delete( p ); }
    //...
};
```

If the intent is to discourage the allocation of arrays of `Handle`s, then the array forms can be declared to be private and left undefined (see *Restricting Heap Allocation* [34, 117]).

A second source of confusion and error concerns the value of the size argument that is passed to array new depending on how the function is called. When `operator new` is called (implicitly) in a new expression, the compiler determines how much memory is required and passes that amount as the first argument to `operator new`. That amount is the size of the object being allocated:

```
aT = new T; // calls operator new( sizeof(T) );
```

It's also possible to call `operator new` directly, in which case we must specify the number of bytes we want to allocate explicitly:

```
aT = static_cast<T *>(operator new( sizeof(T) ));
```

We can also call array new directly:

```
aryT = static_cast<T *>(operator new[]( 5*sizeof(T) ));
```

However, when we call array new implicitly through a new expression, the compiler may, and often does, increase the memory request by a small amount.

```
aryT = new T[5]; // request 5*sizeof(T) + delta bytes
```

The additional space is generally used by the runtime memory manager to record information about the array that is necessary to later reclaim the memory (the number of elements allocated, the size of each element, and so on). To further complicate the situation, the compiler may or may not request this additional space for every allocation, and the size of the request may vary from allocation to allocation.

This difference in the amount requested is typically only a concern in very low-level code, where storage for arrays is being handled directly. If you're going to be low level, it's generally simplest to avoid direct calls to array new and the associated meddling by the compiler and use plain old `operator new` instead (see *Placement New* [35, 119]).

Item 38 | Exception Safety Axioms

Writing an exception safe program or library is a little like proving a theorem in Euclidean geometry. Starting with as minimal a set of axioms as possible, we prove simple theorems. We then use these subsidiary theorems to prove successively more complex and useful theorems. Exception safety is similar, and we build our exception safe code from exception safe components. (Although it's interesting to note that simply composing a set of exception safe components or function calls does not guarantee that the result will be exception safe. That would be too easy, wouldn't it?) As with any proof system, however, we must eventually settle on a set of axioms with which to build our exception safe structure. What are these axioms?

Axiom 1: Exceptions Are Synchronous

First, note that exceptions are synchronous and can occur only at the boundary of a function call. Therefore, operations like arithmetic on predefined types, assignment of predefined types (especially pointers), and other low-level operations will not result in an exception. (They could result in a signal or interrupt of some sort, but these are not exceptions.)

Operator overloading and templates complicate this situation, since it's often difficult to determine whether a given operation will result in a function call and potential exception. For example, if I assign character pointers, I know I won't get an exception, whereas if I assign user-defined `Strings`, I might:

```
const char *a, *b;
String c, d;
//...
a = b; // no function call, no exception
c = d; // function call, maybe an exception
```

With templates, things become less definite:

```
template <typename T>
void aTemplateContext() {
    T e, f;
    T *g, *h;
    //...
    e = f; // function call? exception?
    g = h; // no function call, no exception
    //...
}
```

Because of this uncertainty, all *potential* function calls within a template must be assumed to be actual function calls, and this includes infix operators, implicit conversions, and so on.

Axiom 2: It's Safe to Destroy

This is a socially based, not technically based, axiom. Conventionally, destructors, `operator delete`, and `operator delete[]` do not throw exceptions. Consider an imaginary destructor that must delete two pointer data members. We know that we'll be criticized, ostracized, and marginalized if we allow an exception to propagate from the destructor, so we may be tempted to reach for a try block:

```
X::~X() {
    try {
        delete ptr1_;
        delete ptr2_;
    }
    catch( ... ) {}
}
```

This is not necessary or advisable, since the fear of social ostracism also (one hopes and assumes) affects the authors of the destructors and `operator deletes` of the objects to which `ptr1_` and `ptr2_` refer. We can play on those fears to make our task easier:

```
X::~X() {
    delete ptr1_;
    delete ptr2_;
}
```

Axiom 3: Swap Doesn't Throw

This is another socially based axiom, but it's not as ingrained and universally recognized as the prohibition on destructors and deletions that throw. Swapping would not seem to be a very common operation, but it is used extensively "behind the scenes," most particularly in STL implementations. Whenever you perform a `sort`, `reverse`, `partition`, or any of a large number of other operations, you're swapping, and an exception safe swap goes a long way toward guaranteeing that these operations will be exception safe as well. See also *Copy Operations* [13, 45].

Item 39 Exception Safe Functions

The hard part about writing exception safe code isn't the throwing or catching of exceptions; it's everything in between. As a thrown exception wends its way from the throw expression to the catch clause, every partially executed function on that path must "clean up" any important resources that it controls before its activation record is popped off the execution stack. Generally (but not always), all that is required to write an exception safe function is a moment's reflection and some common sense.

For example, consider the implementation of `String` assignment from *Assignment and Initialization Are Different* [12, 41]:

```
String &String::operator =( const char *str ) {
    if( !str ) str = "";
    char *tmp = strcpy( new char[ strlen(str)+1 ], str );
    delete [] s_;
    s_ = tmp;
    return *this;
}
```

The implementation of this function may look superfluously ornate, since we could have coded it with fewer lines and no temporary:

```
String &String::operator =( const char *str ) {
    delete [] s_;
    if( !str ) str = "";
    s_ = strcpy( new char[ strlen(str)+1 ], str );
    return *this;
}
```

However, while the array delete comes with a social guarantee not to throw an exception (see *Exception Safety Axioms* [38, 131]), the array new a couple of lines later makes no such promise. If we delete the old buffer before we know whether allocation of the new buffer will succeed, we'll leave the String object in a bad state. Herb Sutter summarizes the situation well in his *Exceptional C++*, which I'll paraphrase as this: First do anything that could cause an exception "off to the side" without changing important state, and then use operations that can't throw an exception to finish up. That's what we did in the first implementation of String::operator = above. Let's look at another example from *Commands and Hollywood* [19, 67]:

```
void Button::setAction( const Action *newAction ) {
    Action *temp = newAction->clone(); // off to the side...
    delete action_; // then change state!
    action_ = temp;
}
```

Because it's a virtual function, we really know nothing about the exception-related behavior of the call to clone, so we assume the worst. If the clone operation succeeds, we continue with an exception safe deletion and pointer assignment. Otherwise, a thrown exception from clone will cause premature exit from Button::setAction with no harm done. Newer C++ programmers have a tendency to "clean up" code like this in such a way as to make it exception unsafe:

```
void Button::setAction( const Action *newAction ) {
    delete action_; // change state!
    action_ = newAction->clone(); // then maybe throw?
}
```

Performing the deletion (which is assumed to be exception safe) before the clone (which makes no such promise) will leave the Button object in an inconsistent state if clone throws an exception.

Notice that properly written exception safe code employs relatively few try blocks. A novice attempt to write exception safe code is often littered with unnecessary and often damaging trys and catches:

```
void Button::setAction( const Action *newAction ) {
    delete action_;
    try {
        action_ = newAction->clone();
    }
```

```
    catch( ... ) {
        action_ = 0;
        throw;
    }
}
```

This version with its fussy try block and catch clause is exception safe in the sense that the `Button` object is left in a consistent (but likely different) state if `clone` throws an exception. However, our previous version was shorter, simpler, and more exception safe because it left the `Button` object not merely consistent but unchanged.

It's a good idea to minimize the use of try blocks, where possible, and employ them primarily in locations where you really want to examine the type of a passing exception in order to do something with it. In practice, these locations are often at module boundaries between your code and third-party libraries and between your code and the operating system.

Item 40 RAII

The C++ community has a long and proud tradition of inscrutable abbreviations and odd names for techniques. RAII manages to attain both oddness and inscrutability. RAII stands for "resource acquisition is initialization." (No, not "initialization is resource acquisition," as some would have it. If you're going to be odd, you've got to go all the way or the whole thing falls flat.)

RAII is a simple technique that harnesses C++'s notion of object lifetime to control program resources like memory, file handles, network connections, audit trails, or whatever. The basic technique is simple. If you want to keep track of an important resource, create an object and associate the resource's lifetime with the object's lifetime. In that way, you can use C++'s sophisticated object management facilities to manage resources. In its simplest form, we create an object whose constructor seizes a resource and whose destructor frees the resource.

```
class Resource { ... };
class ResourceHandle {
  public:
    explicit ResourceHandle( Resource *aResource )
        : r_(aResource) {} // seize resource
    ~ResourceHandle()
        { delete r_; } // release resource
    Resource *get()
        { return r_; } // access resource
  private:
    ResourceHandle( const ResourceHandle & );
    ResourceHandle &operator =( const ResourceHandle & );
    Resource *r_;
};
```

The nice thing about a `ResourceHandle` object is that, if it is declared as a local variable of a function, as a function argument, or as a static, we are guaranteed to get a destructor call and recover the resource to which it refers. This is an important property if we want to keep track of our important resources in the face of slapdash maintenance or propagating exceptions. Consider some simple code that doesn't employ RAII:

```
void f() {
    Resource *rh = new Resource;
    //...
    if( iFeelLikeIt() ) // bad maintenance
        return;
    //...
    g(); // exception?
    delete rh; // do we always get here?
}
```

It may be that the original version of this function was safe, and the resource to which `rh` referred was always recovered. However, over time such code tends to break, as less experienced maintainers insert early returns, call functions that can throw an exception, or otherwise avoid the resource recovery code at the end of the function. Use of RAII results in a function that is both simpler and more robust:

```
void f() {
    ResourceHandle rh( new Resource );
    //...
    if( iFeelLikeIt() ) // no problem!
        return;
    //...
    g(); // exception? no problem!
    // rh destructor performs deletion!
}
```

The only time you're not guaranteed a destructor call when using RAII is if the resource handle is allocated on the heap, since the destructor will be called only if the object is deleted explicitly. (In the interests of full disclosure, there are also edge cases where `abort` or `exit` is called and an iffy situation that can occur if a thrown exception is never caught.)

```
ResourceHandle *rhp =
    new ResourceHandle(new Resource); // bad idea!
```

RAII is such a pervasive technique in C++ programming that it's hard to find a library component or significant block of code that does not employ it in some fashion. Note that we have a very broad definition of "resource" that can be controlled via RAII. In addition to resources that are essentially hunks of memory (buffers, strings, container implementations, and the like), we can use RAII to control system resources like file handles, semaphores, and network connections, as well as less glamorous things like login sessions, graphical shapes, or zoo animals.

Consider the following class:

```
class Trace {
  public:
    Trace( const char *msg ) : msg_(msg)
        { std::cout << "Entering " << msg_ << std::endl; }
    ~Trace()
        { std::cout << "Leaving " << msg_ << std::endl; }
  private:
    std::string msg_;
};
```

In the case of `Trace`, the resource we're controlling is a message to be printed when a scope is exited. It's instructive to observe the behavior of a variety of `Trace` objects (automatic, static, local, and global) by following their lifetimes under various types of control flow.

```
void f() {
    Trace tracer( "f" ); // print "entering" message
    ResourceHandle rh( new Resource ); // seize resource
    //...
    if( iFeelLikeIt() ) // no problem!
        return;
    //...
    g(); // exception? no problem!
    // rh destructor performs deletion!
    // tracer destructor prints exiting message!
}
```

The code above also illustrates an important invariant of constructor and destructor structure activation: The activations form a stack. That is, we declared and initialized `tracer` before `rh`, so we are guaranteed that `rh` will be destroyed before `tracer` (last initialized, first destroyed). More generally, whenever we declare a sequence of objects, these objects will be initialized at runtime in a specific order and eventually destroyed in the inverse order. That order of destruction will not vary even in the event of an impromptu `return`, a propagating exception, an unusual `switch`, or an evil `goto`. (If you find this to be a dubious claim, I encourage you to play with the `Trace` class. Very instructive.) This property is particularly important for resource acquisition and release, since it is generally the case that resources must be seized in a particular order and released in the inverse order. For example, a network connection must be opened before an audit message is sent, and a closing audit message must be sent before the connection is closed.

This stack-based behavior extends even into the initialization and destruction of individual objects. An object's constructor initializes its base class subobjects in the order they're declared, followed by its data members in the order that they're declared. Then (and only then) is the body of the constructor executed. Now we know how the object's destructor will behave. Backward. First the destructor body is executed, then the object's data members are destroyed in the inverse order of their declaration, and finally the object's base class subobjects are destroyed in the inverse order of their declaration. In case it's not obvious by this point, this stack-like behavior is really handy for seizing and releasing an object's required resources.

Item 41 New, Constructors, and Exceptions

To write perfectly exception safe code, it's necessary to keep track of any allocated resources and to be prepared to release them if an exception occurs. This is often a straightforward process. We can either organize our code in such a way that no resource recovery is necessary (see *Exception Safe Functions* [39, 135]) or use resource handles to recover the resources automatically (see *RAII* [40, 139]). In extreme situations, we can get down and dirty with try blocks or even nested try blocks, but this should be an exception, not the rule.

We do, however, have an apparent problem with the use of the `new` operator. The `new` operator actually performs two separate operations (see *Placement New* [35, 119]); first it calls a function named `operator new` to allocate some storage, and then it may invoke a constructor to turn that uninitialized storage into an object:

```
String *title = new String( "Kicks" );
```

The problem is that, if an exception occurs, we can't tell whether it was thrown by `operator new` or the `String` constructor. This matters, because if `operator new` succeeds and the constructor throws an exception, we should probably call `operator delete` on the allocated (but uninitialized) storage. If `operator new` was the function that threw the exception, no memory was allocated and we should not call `operator delete`.

One horrible approach is to handcraft the proper behavior by separating the allocation and initialization behavior and tossing in a try block:

```
String *title // allocate raw storage
    = static_cast<String *>(::operator new(sizeof(String));
try {
    new( title ) String( "Kicks" ); // placement new
```

```
}
catch( ... ) {
    ::operator delete( title ); // clean up if ctor throws
}
```

Ouch. So many things are wrong with this code that the approach is not worth considering. In addition to being more trouble for you, the overworked coder, it will not behave properly if `String` has a member `operator new` and `operator delete` (see *Class-Specific Memory Management* [36, 123]). This is a perfect example of too-clever code that works initially but fails subtly in the future because of a remote change (for example, if someone adds `String`-specific memory management).

Fortunately, the compiler handles this situation for us and produces code that performs in the same way as in our hand-coded approach above, but with one exception. It will invoke the `operator delete` that corresponds to the `operator new` used to perform the allocation.

```
String *title = new String( "Kicks" ); // use members if present
String *title = ::new String( "Kicks" ); // use global new/delete
```

In particular, if the allocation uses a member `operator new`, then the corresponding member `operator delete` will be called to reclaim the storage if the `String` constructor throws an exception. This is yet another good reason to declare a member `operator delete` if you declare a member `operator new`.

Essentially the same situation applies to array allocation and allocations that use overloaded versions of `operator new[]`; the compiler will attempt to find and call the appropriate `operator delete[]`.

Item 42 | Smart Pointers

We C++ programmers are a loyal bunch. Whenever we're faced with a situation that requires a feature the language doesn't support, we don't abandon C++ to flirt with some other language; we just extend C++ to support the feature in which we're interested.

For instance, it's often the case that you'll need something that behaves like a pointer, but a built-in pointer type just doesn't do the job. In those cases, a C++ programmer will use a "smart pointer." (See also *Function Objects* [18, 63] for similar observations about function pointers.)

A smart pointer is a class type that is tricked up to look and act like a pointer but that provides additional capability beyond that provided by a built-in pointer. Generally, a smart pointer uses the capabilities provided by a class's constructors, destructor, and copy operations to control access to or keep track of what it points to in a way that a built-in pointer cannot.

All smart pointers overload the `->` and `*` operators so that they can be used with standard pointer syntax. (Some rare specimens even go so far as to overload the `->*` operator; see *Pointers to Class Members Are Not Pointers* [15, 53].) Other smart pointers (in particular, smart pointers used as STL iterators) overload other pointer operators, like `++`, `--`, `+`, `-`, `+=`, `-=`, and `[]`(see *Pointer Arithmetic* [44, 149]). Smart pointers are often implemented as class templates so that they may refer to different types of objects. Here's a very simple smart pointer template that performs a check that it's not null before use:

```
template <typename T>
class CheckedPtr {
  public:
    explicit CheckedPtr( T *p ) : p_( p ) {}
    ~CheckedPtr() { delete p_; }
    T *operator ->() { return get(); }
    T &operator *() { return *get(); }
  private:
    T *p_; // what we're pointing to
```

```
    T *get() { // check ptr before returning it
        if( !p_ )
            throw NullCheckedPointer();
        return p_;
    }
    CheckedPtr( const CheckedPtr & );
    CheckedPtr &operator =( const CheckedPtr & );
};
```

Use of a smart pointer should be straightforward, mimicking the use of a built-in pointer:

```
CheckedPtr<Shape> s( new Circle );
s->draw(); // same as (s.operator ->())->draw()
```

The key to this façade is the overloaded `operator ->`. The `->` operator must be overloaded as a member and has a rather unusual property in that it is not "consumed" when it is called. In other words, when we write `s->draw()`, the compiler recognizes that `s` is not a pointer but a class object with an overloaded `operator ->` (that is, that `s` is a smart pointer). This results in a call to the member overloaded operator, which returns (in this case) a `Shape *` built-in pointer. This pointer is then used to call `Shape`'s `draw` function. If you write this out longhand, you'll get the following challenging expression: `(s.operator ->())->draw()`, which contains two uses of the `->` operator, one overloaded, one built in.

Smart pointers also typically overload `operator *` as well as `operator ->` so that they may be used to refer to nonclass types.

```
CheckedPtr<int> ip = new int;
*ip = 12; // same as ip.operator *() = 12
(*s).draw(); // use on ptr to class, too
```

Smart pointers are used pervasively in C++ programming, from resource handles (see *RAII* [40, 139] and *auto_ptr Is Unusual* [43, 147]) to STL iterators, to reference counting pointers, to wrappers around pointers to member functions, and on and on. *Semper fidelis.*

Item 43 | auto_ptr Is Unusual

Whenever one discusses RAII, it's necessary to discuss auto_ptr. This is always a task. It's not that we're ashamed of auto_ptr, mind you, but it's kind of like explaining your brother to strangers; he's a superlative person, but you have to be in the right frame of mind to appreciate that. And there's no denying that both your brother and auto_ptr have a different worldview from the typical person or object, respectively.

As we discussed in *RAII* [40, 139], the use of resource handles is a pervasively employed technique in C++ programming, so the standard library supplies a resource handle template that serves many resource handle needs: auto_ptr. The auto_ptr class template is used to generate smart pointers (see *Smart Pointers* [42, 145]) that know how to clean up after themselves.

```
using std::auto_ptr; // see Namespaces [23, 81]
auto_ptr<Shape> aShape( new Circle );
aShape->draw(); // draw a circle
(*aShape).draw(); // draw it again
```

Like all well-designed smart pointers, auto_ptr overloads operator -> and operator * so that you can usually pretend you're dealing with a built-in pointer. There are many nice things about auto_ptr. First, it's very efficient. You're not likely to get better performance with a hand-coded solution that uses a built-in pointer. Second, when an auto_ptr goes out of scope, its destructor will free whatever it's pointing to, just as our hand-coded resource handle did. In the code fragment above, the Circle object to which aShape refers will be (effectively) garbage collected.

A third nice thing about auto_ptr is that it behaves like a built-in pointer with respect to conversions:

```
auto_ptr<Circle> aCircle( new Circle );
aShape = aCircle;
```

Through its clever use of template member functions (see *Member Templates* [50, 173]) one auto_ptr can be copied to another if the corresponding built-in pointers could. In the code above, an auto_ptr<Circle> can be assigned to an auto_ptr<Shape> because a Circle * can be assigned to a Shape * (assuming that Shape is a public base class of Circle).

Where auto_ptr differs from the typical smart pointer (or typical object, for that matter) is in its copy operations. For a typical class, the copy operations (see *Copy Operations* [13, 45]) will not affect the source of the copy. In other words, if T is some type

```
T a;
T b( a ); // copy construction of b with a
a = b; // assignment from b to a
```

then when b is initialized with a, the value of a is unaffected, and when b is assigned to a, the value of b is unaffected. Not so with auto_ptr! When we assigned aCircle to aShape above, both source and target of the assignment were affected. If aShape was non-null, whatever it referred to was deleted and replaced with what aCircle pointed to. In addition, aCircle was set to null. Assignment and initialization of auto_ptrs are not really copy operations; they are operations that transfer control of the underlying object from one auto_ptr to another. One can think of the right argument of an assignment or initialization as a "source" and the left argument as a "sink." Control of the underlying object is passed from source to sink. This is a good property in a resource handle.

However, one should avoid the use of auto_ptrs in two common situations. First, they should never be used as container elements. Container elements are often copied around within a container, and the container will assume that its elements obey the usual, non-auto_ptr copy semantics. Feel free to use a smart pointer as a container element, just as long as it's not an auto_ptr. Second, an auto_ptr should refer to a single element, not an array. The reason is that when the object to which the auto_ptr refers is deleted, it will be deleted using operator delete, not array delete. If the auto_ptr refers to an array, the wrong deletion operator will be called (see *Array Allocation* [37, 127]).

```
vector< auto_ptr<Shape> > shapes; // likely error, bad idea
auto_ptr<int> ints( new int[32] ); // bad idea, no error (yet)
```

Generally, a standard vector or string is a reasonable alternative to an auto_ptr to an array.

Item 44 Pointer Arithmetic

Pointer arithmetic is straightforward. To understand the nature of pointer arithmetic in C++, it's best to consider a pointer into an array:

```
const int MAX = 10;
short points[MAX];
short *curPoint = points+4;
```

This gives us an array and a pointer to somewhere near the middle of the array, as shown in Figure 9.

If we increment or decrement the pointer `curPoint`, we are requesting that it point to the next or previous `short` in the `points` array. In other words, pointer arithmetic is always scaled in the size of the object that is being pointed to; incrementing `curPoint` by one does not add a one byte to the address in the pointer—it adds `sizeof(short)` bytes. This is why there is no pointer arithmetic available on `void *` pointers; we don't know what type of object the `void *` refers to, so we can't scale the arithmetic properly.

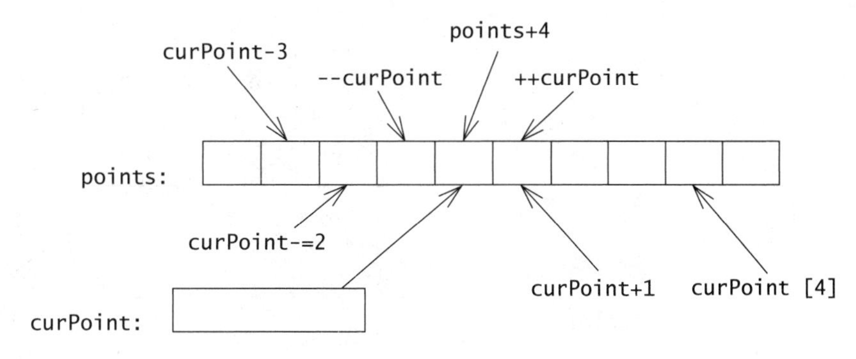

Figure 9 Effect of various arithmetic operations on the address contained in a pointer

The only time this simple scheme seems to cause confusion is in the case of multidimensional arrays, because novice C++ programmers tend to forget that a multidimensional array is an array of arrays:

```
const int ROWS = 2;
const int COLS = 3;
int table[ROWS][COLS]; // array of ROWS arrays of COLS ints
int (*ptable)[COLS] = table; // ptr to array of COLS ints
```

It's convenient to visualize the two-dimensional array shown in Figure 10 as a table even though it's actually laid out in a linear fashion in memory, as illustrated in Figure 11.

When we perform pointer arithmetic on `ptable`, the arithmetic is, as always, scaled in the size of the object to which `ptable` points. But that object is an array of `COLS` `ints` (which is `sizeof(int)*COLS` bytes), not an `int`.

table:

0,0	0,1	0,2
1,0	1,1	1,2

Figure 10 | A two-dimensional array is conceptually a table.

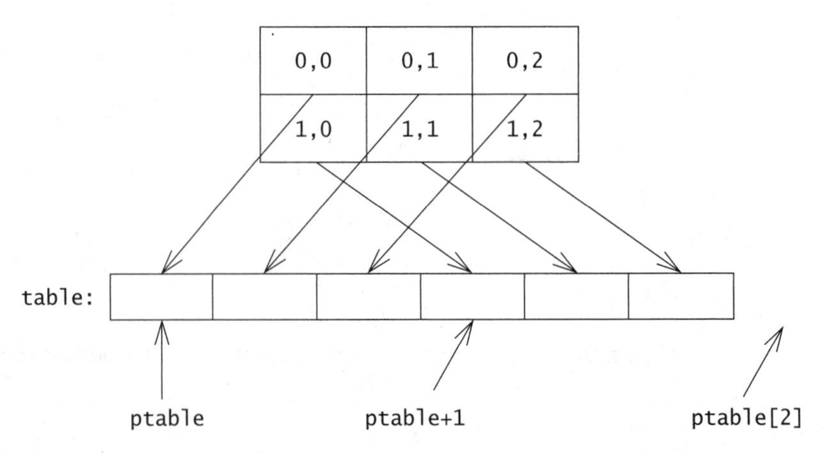

Figure 11 | A two-dimensional array is actually a linear sequence of one-dimensional arrays.

Pointers of the same type may be subtracted. The result is the number of objects (not the number of bytes) that lie between the two pointers. If the first pointer is greater (refers to a higher memory location) than the second pointer, the result is positive; otherwise it's negative. If the two pointers refer to the same object, or are both null, the result is zero. The type of the result of subtracting two pointers is the standard typedef `ptrdiff_t`, which is usually an alias for `int`. Two pointers may not be added, multiplied, or divided, because these operations just don't make conventional sense for addresses. Pointers are not integers (but see *Placement New* [35, 119]).

This commonly understood concept of pointer arithmetic is used as a metaphor for the design of STL iterators (see *The Standard Template Library* [4, 11] and *Smart Pointers* [42, 145]). STL iterators also permit pointer-like arithmetic that employs the same syntax as built-in pointers. In fact, built-in pointers are compliant STL iterators. Consider a possible implementation of an STL list container, as shown in Figure 12:

This configuration could have come about by executing the following code:

```
int a[] = { 1, 2, 3, 4 };
std::list<int> lst( a, a+4 );
std::list<int>::iterator iter = lst.begin();
++iter;
```

A `list`'s iterator cannot be a built-in pointer but is instead a smart pointer with overloaded operators. The pointer arithmetic-like operation `++iter` does not increment `iter` the way it would increment a pointer; instead, it follows a link from the current node of the list to the next. However, the analogy with arithmetic on built-in pointers is exact; the increment operation moves the iterator to the next element in the list, the way incrementing a built-in pointer moves it to the next element of an array.

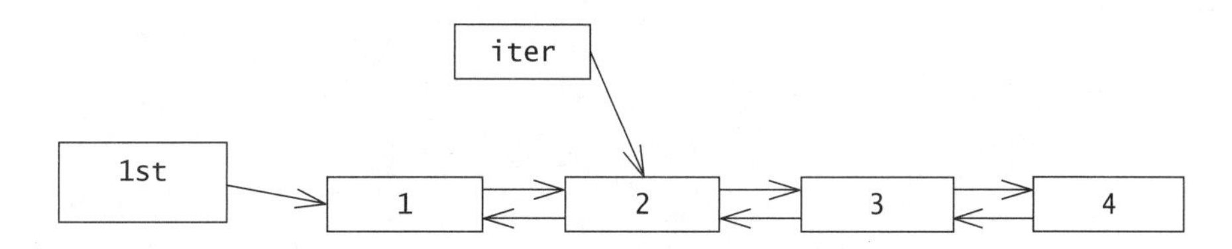

Figure 12 Possible implementation of a standard list. A list iterator isn't a pointer, but it is modeled on a pointer.

Item 45 Template Terminology

Precise use of terminology is always important in any technical field, particularly in programming, most particularly in C++ programming, and most definitely particularly in C++ template programming.

Figure 13 illustrates the most important aspects of C++ template terminology.

Be particularly careful to distinguish between a template parameter, which is used in the declaration of a template, and template argument, which is used in the specialization of a template.

```
template <typename T> // T is a template parameter
class Heap { ... };
//...
Heap<double> dHeap; // double is a template argument
```

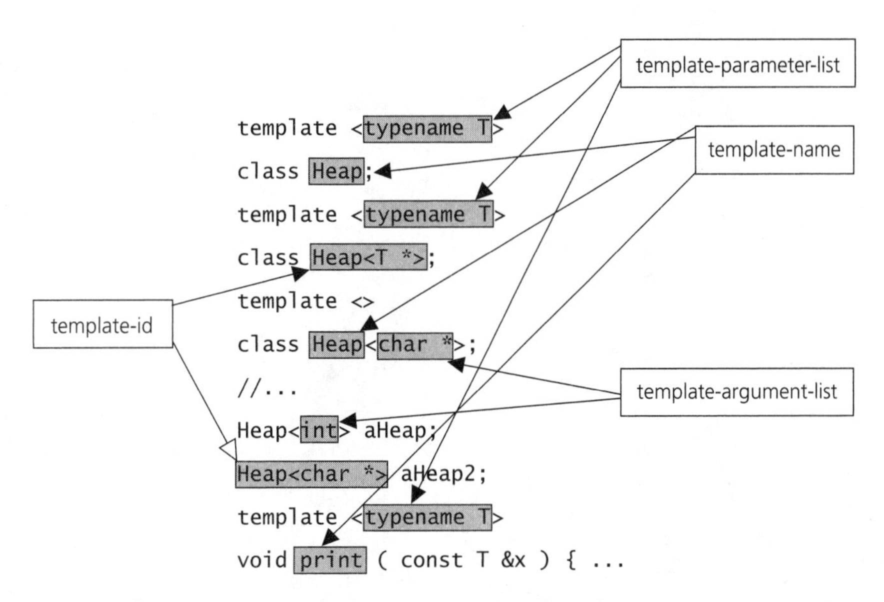

Figure 13 | Template terminology. Precise use of terminology is essential to precise communication of a template design.

Also be careful to distinguish between a template-name, which is a simple identifier, and a template-id, which is a template name with an appended template argument list.

Most C++ programmers confuse the terms "instantiation" and "specialization." A specialization of a template is what you get when you supply a template with a set of template arguments. The specialization can be implicit or explicit. For example, when we write `Heap<int>`, we are explicitly specializing the `Heap` class template with an `int` argument. When we write `print( 12.3 )`, we are implicitly specializing the `print` function template with a `double` argument. A specialization of a template may or may not cause a template instantiation. For example, if there is a customized version of `Heap` for `int` available, the specialization `Heap<int>` will refer to that version and no instantiation will take place (see *Class Template Explicit Specialization* [46, 155]). However, if the primary `Heap` template is used, or if a partial specialization is used (see *Template Partial Specialization* [47, 161]), then an instantiation will take place.

Item 46 Class Template Explicit Specialization

Class template explicit specialization is straightforward. First, you need a general case to specialize. This general case is called the "primary" template.

```
template <typename T> class Heap;
```

The primary template has only to be declared to be specialized (as `Heap` is above), but it is usually also defined (as `Heap` is below):

```
template <typename T>
class Heap {
  public:
    void push( const T &val );
    T pop();
    bool empty() const { return h_.empty(); }
  private:
    std::vector<T> h_;
};
```

Our primary template implements a heap data structure by putting an easy-to-use interface around the somewhat challenging standard library heap algorithms. A heap is a linearized tree structure that is optimized for insertion and retrieval. Pushing a value into a heap inserts the value into the tree structure, and popping a heap removes and returns the largest value in the heap. For example, the `push` and `pop` operations can be implemented using the standard `push_heap` and `pop_heap` algorithms:

```
template <typename T>
void Heap<T>::push( const T &val ) {
    h_.push_back(val);
    std::push_heap( h_.begin(), h_.end() );
}

template <typename T>
```

```
T Heap<T>::pop() {
    std::pop_heap( h_.begin(), h_.end() );
    T tmp( h_.back() );
    h_.pop_back();
    return tmp;
}
```

This implementation works well for many types of values but falls down in the case of pointers to characters. By default, the standard heap algorithms use the < operator to compare and organize the elements in the heap. In the case of pointers to characters, however, this would result in the heap's being organized according to the addresses of the strings to which the character pointers refer, not the values of the strings themselves. That is, the heap will be organized by the values of the pointers, not the values of what they point to.

We can address this particular difficulty with an explicit specialization of the primary `Heap` template for pointers to character:

```
template <>
class Heap<const char *> {
  public:
    void push( const char *pval );
    const char *pop();
    bool empty() const { return h_.empty(); }
  private:
    std::vector<const char *> h_;
};
```

The template-parameter-list is empty, but the template argument for which we're specializing is appended to the template-name. Curiously, this class template explicit specialization is not a template, because there is no template parameter left unspecified. For this reason, a class template explicit specialization is commonly called a "complete specialization" to distinguish it from a partial specialization, which *is* a template (see *Template Partial Specialization* [47, 161]).

The technical terminology in this area is tricky: A template specialization is a template name with template arguments supplied (see *Template Terminology* [45, 153]). The syntax `Heap<const char *>` is a template specialization, as is `Heap<int>`. However, the first specialization of `Heap` will not result in an instantiation of the Heap template (because the explicit specialization defined for const char * will be used), but the second specialization will cause the primary Heap template to be instantiated.

The implementation of the specialization can be customized to the needs of the const char * element type. For example, the push operation can insert a new value into the heap based on the value of the string to which the pointer refers, rather than the address contained in the pointer:

```
bool strLess( const char *a, const char *b )
    { return strcmp( a, b ) < 0; }

void Heap<const char *>::push( const char *pval ) {
    h_.push_back(pval);
    std::push_heap( h_.begin(), h_.end(), strLess );
}
```

Note the absence of the template keyword and parameter list in the definition of Heap<const char *>::push; this is not a function template because, as we noted above, the explicit specialization Heap<const char *> is not a template.

With the availability of this complete specialization, we can distinguish between Heaps of const char *s and other Heaps:

```
Heap<int> h1; // use primary template
Heap<const char *> h2; // use explicit specialization
Heap<char *> h3; // use primary template!
```

The compiler checks a class template specialization against the declaration of the primary template. If the template arguments match the primary template (in the case of Heap, if there is a single type name argument) the compiler will look for an explicit specialization that matches the template arguments exactly. If we want to special case for Heaps of char * in addition to Heaps of const char *, we have to provide an additional explicit specialization:

```
template <>
class Heap<char *> {
  public:
    void push( char *pval );
```

```
    char *pop();
    size_t size() const;
    void capitalize();
    // no empty!
  private:
    std::vector<char *> h_;
};
```

Notice that there is no requirement that an explicit specialization's interface match that of the primary template. For example, in the case of our first explicit specialization of `Heap` for `const char *`, the formal argument type of the `push` function was declared to be `const char *` rather than `const char *&`. This is a reasonable optimization for a pointer argument. In the case of the specialization of `Heap` for `char *`, we've gone even further in departing from the interface of the primary template.

We've added two new functions (`size` and `capitalize`), which is both legal and sometimes useful, and not provided another (`empty`), which is legal but generally inadvisable. When considering the interfaces of class template explicit specializations, it's helpful to make an analogy to the relationship between base and derived classes (though class template explicit specialization has absolutely no technical connection to class derivation). Users of a class hierarchy often write polymorphic code to the base class interface with the expectation that the derived class will implement that interface (see *Polymorphism* [2, 3]). Similarly, users will often write generic code to the interface provided in the primary template (if the primary is defined as well as declared) and will expect that any specialization will have at least those capabilities (though, as with a derived class, it may have additional capabilities). Consider a simple function template:

```
template <typename T, typename Out>
void extractHeap( Heap<T> &h, Out dest ) {
    while( !h.empty() )
        *dest++ = h.pop();
}
```

The author of this function template will have unkind thoughts about the author of the `char *` explicit specialization of `Heap` if this code works:

```
Heap<const char *> heap1;
//...
vector<const char *> vec1;
extractHeap( heap1, back_inserter(vec1) ); // fine...
```

and this code fails to compile:

```
Heap<char *> heap2;
//...
vector<char *> vec2;
extractHeap( heap2, back_inserter(vec2) ); // error! no empty
```

Item 47 Template Partial Specialization

Let's get it straight: you can't partially specialize function templates. It's just not a part of the C++ language (although it may be some day). What you probably want to do is overload them (see *Overloading Function Templates* [58, 213]). Accordingly, we are considering only class templates in this item.

The way class template partial specialization works is straightforward. As with complete specialization, you first need a general case—or primary template—to specialize. Let's use our `Heap` template from *Class Template Explicit Specialization* [46, 155]:

```
template <typename T> class Heap;
```

Explicit specialization (also known colloquially as "complete" specialization) is used to customize a class template for a precise set of arguments. In *Class Template Explicit Specialization* [46, 155], we used it to provide customized implementations of `Heap` for `const char *` and `char *`. However, we still have a problem with `Heaps` of other pointer types, in that we'd like to order the `Heap` according to the values to which the pointer elements refer, rather than the value of the pointers themselves.

```
Heap<double *> readings; // primary template, T is double *
```

Because the type (`double *`) does not match either of our character pointer complete specializations, the compiler will instantiate the primary template. We could provide complete specializations for `double *` and every other pointer type of interest, but this is onerous and ultimately unmaintainable. This is a job for partial specialization:

```
template <typename T>
class Heap<T *> {
  public:
    void push( const T *val );
    T *pop();
```

```
    bool empty() const { return h_.empty(); }
  private:
    std::vector<T *> h_;
};
```

The syntax of a partial specialization is similar to that of a complete specialization, but the template parameter list is not empty. Like a complete specialization, the class template name is a template-id and not a simple template name (see *Template Terminology* [45, 153]).

This partial specialization for pointers allows us to modify the implementation appropriately. For example, insertions can be made based on the value of the object pointed to, rather than the value of the pointer. First, let's whip up a comparator that compares two pointers by the values of what they point to (see *STL Function Objects* [20, 71]):

```
template <typename T>
struct PtrCmp : public std::binary_function<T *, T *, bool> {
    bool operator ()( const T *a, const T *b ) const
        { return *a < *b; }
};
```

Now let's use our comparator to implement a `push` operation with the correct behavior:

```
template <typename T>
void Heap<T *>::push( T *pval ) {
    if( pval ) {
        h_.push_back(pval);
        std::push_heap( h_.begin(), h_.end(), PtrCmp<T>() );
    }
}
```

Note that, unlike a complete specialization of a class template, a partial specialization is a template, and the `template` keyword and parameter list are required in definitions of its members.

Unlike our complete specializations, the parameter type of this version of `Heap` is not completely determined; it's only partially determined to be `T *`, where `T` is an unspecified type. That's what makes it a partial specialization. This partial specialization will be preferred to the primary template when instantiating a `Heap` with any (unqualified) pointer type. Further, the complete specializations of `Heap` for `const char *` and `char *` will be preferred to this partial specialization if the template argument type is `const char *` or `char *`.

```
Heap<std::string> h1; // primary, T is std::string
Heap<std::string *> h2; // partial spec, T is std::string
Heap<int **> h3; // partial spec, T is int *
Heap<char *> h4; // complete spec for char *
Heap<char **> h5; // partial spec, T is char *
Heap<const int *> h6; // partial spec, T is const int
Heap<int (*)()> h7; // partial spec, T is int ()
```

The complete set of rules for choosing among the various available partial specializations is rather involved, but most cases are straightforward. Generally, the most specific, most restricted candidate is chosen. The partial specialization mechanism is precise and allows us to select among candidates with high precision. For example, we could augment our set of partial specializations with one for pointers to const:

```
template <typename T>
class Heap<const T *> {
  //...
};
//...
Heap<const int *> h6; // different partial spec, now T is int
```

Note that, as we discussed in *Class Template Explicit Specialization* [46, 155], the compiler checks a class template specialization against the declaration of the primary template. If the template arguments match the primary template (in the case of `Heap`, if there is a single type name argument) the compiler will look for the complete or partial specialization that best matches the template arguments.

Here's a subtle and useful point: A complete or partial specialization of a primary template must be instantiated with the same number and kind of arguments as the primary, but its template parameter list does not have to have the same form as that of the primary. In the case of `Heap`, the primary takes a single type name parameter, so any complete or partial specialization of `Heap` must be instantiated with a single type name argument:

```
template <typename T> class Heap;
```

Therefore, a complete specialization of `Heap` still takes a single type name template argument, but the template parameter list differs from that of the primary because it is empty:

```
template <> class Heap<char *>;
```

A partial specialization of `Heap` must also take a single type name template argument, and its template parameter list may have a single type name parameter in its template header

```
template <typename T> class Heap<T *>;
```

but it doesn't have to.

```
template <typename T, int n> class Heap<T [n]>;
```

This partial specialization will be selected for a specialization of `Heap` with an array type. For example:

```
Heap<float *[6]> h8; // partial spec, T is float * and n is 6
```

Essentially, this partial specialization says, "This partial specialization takes a single type parameter like the primary template, but that parameter must have the form 'array of `T` of size `n`.'" Consider some more involved examples:

```
template <typename R, typename A1, typename A2>
class Heap<R (*)(A1,A2)>;

template <class C, typename T>
class Heap<T C::*>;
```

With the addition of these partial specializations, we can special case for `Heap`s of pointers to non-member functions that take two arguments and `Heap`s of pointers to data members (though why you'd want heaps of these things is anybody's guess):

```
Heap<char *(*)(int,int)> h9; // partial spec
                             // R is char *, A1 and A2 are int
Heap<std::string Name::*> h10; // partial spec
                               // T is string, C is Name
```

Item 48 | Class Template Member Specialization

A common misconception about class template explicit specialization and partial specialization is that a specialization somehow "inherits" something from the primary template. This is not the case. A complete or partial specialization of a class template is a totally separate entity from the primary template and does not "inherit" either interface or implementation from the primary template. However, in a nontechnical sense, specializations do inherit a set of expectations about their interfaces and behaviors, in that users who write generic code to the interface of a primary template generally expect that code to work with specializations as well.

This implies that a complete or partial specialization must generally reimplement all the capabilities of the primary template, even if only a portion of the implementation requires customization. An alternative is often to specialize only a subset of the primary template's member functions. For example, consider the primary `Heap` template (see *Class Template Explicit Specialization* [46, 155]):

```
template <typename T>
class Heap {
  public:
    void push( const T &val );
    T pop();
    bool empty() const { return h_.empty(); }
  private:
    std::vector<T> h_;
};
```

Our complete specialization of `Heap` for `const char *` replaced the entire implementation of the primary, even though its private implementation and `empty` member function were perfectly adequate for a heap of character pointers. All we really had to do was specialize the `push` and `pop` member functions:

```
template <>
void Heap<const char *>::push( const char *const &pval ) {
    h_.push_back(pval);
    std::push_heap( h_.begin(), h_.end(), strLess );
}

template<>
const char *Heap<const char *>::pop() {
    std::pop_heap( h_.begin(), h_.end(), strLess );
    const char *tmp = h_.back(); h_.pop_back();
    return tmp;
}
```

These functions are explicit specializations of the corresponding members of the primary `Heap` template and will be used in place of the implicitly instantiated versions for `Heap<const char *>`.

Note that the interface of each of these functions must match exactly the corresponding interface in the template whose members they're specializing. For example, the primary template declared `push` to take an argument of type `const T &`, so the explicit specialization of `push` for `const char *` must have an argument type of `const char * const &`. (That's a reference to a const pointer to a const char.) Note that we didn't have this restriction when providing a complete specialization of the `Heap` template as a whole, where the argument to `push` was declared to be simply `const char *`.

To increase the level of complexity (a common occurrence when programming with templates), let's consider what would happen if we had available our partial specialization of `Heap` for pointers in general (see *Template Partial Specialization* [47, 161]):

```
template <typename T>
class Heap<T *> {
    //...
    void push( T *pval );
    //...
};
```

If this partial specialization of `Heap` is present, our explicit specialization of `push` now must conform to the interface of the `push` member of the partial specialization, since that's the function that would otherwise be instantiated for `Heap<const char *>`. The explicit specialization must now be declared as follows:

```
template <>
void Heap<const char *>::push( const char *pval ) {
    h_.push_back(pval);
    std::push_heap( h_.begin(), h_.end(), strLess );
}
```

Two final notes: First, other members of class templates may be explicitly specialized in addition to member functions, including static members and member templates.

Second, there is often confusion about the difference between explicit specialization and explicit instantiation. As we've seen in this item, explicit specialization is a means of providing a custom version of a template or template member that differs from what one would have gotten from an implicit instantiation. Explicit instantiation simply tells the compiler, explicitly, to instantiate a member that is identical to what one would have gotten with an implicit instantiation.

```
template void Heap<double>::push( const double & );
```

See also *You Instantiate What You Use* [61, 225].

Item 49 | Disambiguating with Typename

Even experienced C++ programmers are often put off by the rather complex syntax required to program with templates. Of all the syntactic gyrations one has to undertake, none is more initially confusing than the occasional need to help the compiler disambiguate a parse.

As an example, let's look at a portion of an implementation of a simple, nonstandard container template.

```
template <typename T>
class PtrList {
  public:
    //...
    typedef T *ElemT;
    void insert( ElemT );
    //...
};
```

It's common practice for class templates to embed information about themselves as nested type names. This allows us to access information about the instantiated template through the appropriate nested name (see *Embedded Type Information* [53, 189] and *Traits* [54, 193]).

```
typedef PtrList<State> StateList;
//...
StateList::ElemT currentState = 0;
```

The nested name `ElemT` allows us easy access to what the `PtrList` template considers to be its element type. Even though we instantiated `PtrList` with the type name `State`, the element type is `State *`. In other circumstances, `PtrList` could be implemented with a smart pointer element type, or a very sophisticated implementation of `PtrList` might vary its implementation based on the properties of the type used to instantiate it (see *Specializing for Type Information* [52, 183]). Use of the nested type name helps to insulate users of `PtrList` from these internal implementation decisions.

Here's another nonstandard container:

```
template <typename Etype>
class SCollection {
  public:
    //...
    typedef Etype ElemT;
    void insert( const Etype & );
    //...
};
```

It appears that `SCollection` is designed according to the same set of naming standards as `PtrList`, in that it also defines a nested `ElemT` type name. Adherence to an established convention is useful, because (among other advantages) it allows us to write generic algorithms that work with a range of different container types. For example, we could write a simple utility algorithm that fills a conforming container with the content of an array of the appropriate element type:

```
template <class Cont>
void fill( Cont &c, Cont::ElemT a[], int len ) { // error!
    for( int i = 0; i < len; ++i )
        c.insert( a[i] );
}
```

Unfortunately, we have a syntax error. The nested name `Cont::ElemT` is not recognized as a type name! The trouble is that, in the context of the `fill` template, the compiler does not have enough information to determine whether the nested name `ElemT` is a type name or a nontype name. The standard says that in such situations, the nested name is assumed to be a nontype name.

If at first this makes no sense to you, you're not alone. However, let's see what information is available to the compiler in different contexts. First, let's consider the situation in which we have a nontemplate class:

```
class MyContainer {
  public:
    typedef State ElemT;
    //...
};
//...
MyContainer::ElemT *anElemPtr = 0;
```

There's clearly no problem here, since the compiler can examine the content of the `MyContainer` class, verify that it has a member named `ElemT`, and note that `MyContainer::ElemT` is indeed a type name. Things are just as simple for a class that is generated from a class template.

```
typedef PtrList<State> StateList;
//...
StateList::ElemT aState = 0;
PtrList<State>::ElemT anotherState = 0;
```

To the compiler, an instantiated class template is just a class, and there is no difference in the access of a nested name from the class type `PtrList<State>` than there is from `MyContainer`. In either case, the compiler just examines the content of the class to determine whether `ElemT` is a type name.

However, once we enter the context of a template, things are different because there is less precise information available. Consider the following fragment:

```
template <typename T>
void aFuncTemplate( T &arg ) {
    ...T::ElemT...
```

When the compiler encounters the qualified name `T::ElemT`, what does it know? From the template parameter list it knows that `T` is a type name of some sort. It can also determine that `T` is a class name because we've employed the scope operator (`::`) to access a nested name of `T`. But that's all the compiler knows, because there is no information available about the content of `T`. For instance, we could call `aFuncTemplate` with a `PtrList`, in which case `T::ElemT` would be a type name.

```
PtrList<State> states;
//...
aFuncTemplate( states ); // T::ElemT is PtrList<State>::ElemT
```

But what if we were to instantiate `aFuncTemplate` with a different type?

```
struct X {
    enum Types { typeA, typeB, typeC } ElemT;
    //...
};
X anX;
//...
```

```
aFuncTemplate( anX ); // T::ElemT is X::ElemT
```

In this case, `T::ElemT` is the name of a data member—a nontype name. What's a compiler to do? The standard tossed a coin, and in cases where it can't determine the type of a nested name, the compiler will assume the nested name is a nontype name. That is the cause of the syntax error in the `fill` function template above.

To deal with this situation, we must sometimes explicitly inform the compiler when a nested name is a type name.

```
template <typename T>
void aFuncTemplate( T &arg ) {
    ...typename T::ElemT...
```

Here we've used the `typename` keyword to tell the compiler explicitly that the following qualified name is a type name. This allows the compiler to parse the template correctly. Note that we are telling the compiler that `ElemT` is a type name, not `T`. The compiler can already determine that `T` is a type name. Similarly, if we were to write

```
typename A::B::C::D::E
```

we'd be telling the compiler that the (very) nested name `E` is a type name.

Of course, if `aFuncTemplate` is instantiated with a type that does not satisfy the requirements of the parsed template, it will result in a compile-time error.

```
struct Z {
    // no member named ElemT...
};
Z aZ;
//...
aFuncTemplate( aZ ); // error! no member Z::ElemT
aFuncTemplate( anX ); // error! X::ElemT is not a type name
aFuncTemplate( states ); // OK. nested ElemT is a type
```

Now we can rewrite the `fill` function template to parse correctly:

```
template <class Cont>
void fill( Cont &c, typename Cont::ElemT a[], int len ) { // OK
    for( int i = 0; i < len; ++i )
        c.insert( a[i] );
}
```

Item 50 | Member Templates

Class templates have members that are not themselves templates, and many of these members can be defined outside the class. Let's look at a singly linked list container:

```
template <typename T>
class SList {
  public:
    SList() : head_(0) {}
    //...
    void push_front( const T &val );
    void pop_front();
    T front() const;
    void reverse();
    bool empty() const;
  private:
    struct Node {
        Node *next_;
        T el_;
    };
    Node *head_; // -> list
};
```

The member functions of a template, when defined outside the class template, have a template header with the same structure as that used in the class template definition:

```
template <typename T>
bool SList<T>::empty() const
    { return head_ == 0; }
```

We've decided to implement our singly linked list as a pointer to a sequence of nodes, where each node contains a list element and a pointer to the next node on the list. (A more sophisticated implementation might embed a truncated `Node` in the `SList`, rather than a pointer to a `Node`, but this is sufficient for our needs here.) Generally, such a nested class type is defined within the template itself, but it needn't be:

```
template <typename T>
class SList {
  public:
    //...
  private:
    struct Node; // incomplete class declaration
    Node *head_; // -> list
    //...
};

template <typename T> // definition outside template
struct SList<T>::Node {
    Node *next_;
    T el_;
};
```

The members `empty` and `Node` are examples of template members. But a class template (or even a nontemplate class) can also have member templates. (Yes, we are witnessing yet another example of C++'s penchant for defining easily confused technical terms. This little gem joins with the `new` operator/`operator new`, covariance/contravariance, and `const_iterator`/const iterator pairs to ensure that every design review will be an adventure.) In the finest tautological tradition, a member template is a member that is a template:

```
template <typename T>
class SList {
  public:
    //...
    template <typename In> SList( In begin, In end );
    //...
};
```

This `SList` constructor, unlike the default constructor, is a member template, explicitly parameterized with the typename `In`. It's also implicitly parameterized by the type name used to instantiate the `SList` template of which it is a member. This explains the highly repetitious nature of its definition when it's defined outside its class template:

```
template <typename T> // this one's for SList
template <typename In> // this one's for the member
SList<T>::SList( In begin, In end ) : head_( 0 ) {
    while( begin != end )
        push_front( *begin++ );
    reverse();
}
```

As with other function templates, the compiler will perform argument deduction and instantiate the constructor template as needed (see *Template Argument Deduction* [57, 209]):

```
float rds[] = { ... };
const int size = sizeof(rds)/sizeof(rds[0]);
std::vector<double> rds2( rds, rds+size );
//...
SList<float> data( rds, rds+size ); // In is float *
SList<double> data2( rds2.begin(), rds2.end() ); // In is
                                    // vector<double>::iterator
```

This is a common use of constructor templates in the STL to allow a container to be initialized by a sequence of values drawn from an arbitrary source. Another common use of member templates is to generate copy operation–like constructors and assignment operators:

```
template <typename T>
class SList {
  public:
    //...
    template <typename S>
        SList( const SList<S> &that );
    template <typename S>
        SList &operator =( const SList<S> &rhs );
    //...
};
```

These template members can be used for copy constructor–like and copy assignment–like operations.

```
SList<double> data3( data ); // T is double, S is float
data = data3; // T is float, S is double
```

Notice the waffle words "copy constructor–like" and "copy assignment–like" in the above description. This is because a template member is never used to instantiate a copy operation; that is, if `T` and `S` are the same type above, then the compiler will not instantiate the member template but will instead write the copy operation itself. In such cases, it's usually best to define the copy operations explicitly in order to forestall officious and often incorrect help from the compiler:

```
template <typename T>
class SList {
  public:
    //...
    SList( const SList &that ); // copy ctor
    SList &operator =( const SList &rhs ); // copy assignment
    template <typename S> SList( const SList<S> &that );
    template <typename S>
        SList &operator =( const SList<S> &rhs );
    //...
};
//...
SList<float> data4( data ); // copy ctor
data3 = data2; // copy assignment
data3 = data4; // non-copy assignment from member template
```

Any nonvirtual member function may be a template (member templates can't be virtual because the combination of these features results in insurmountable technical problems in their implementation). For example, we could implement a sort operation for our list:

```
template <typename T>
class SList {
  public:
    //...
    template <typename Comp> void sort( Comp comp );
    //...
};
```

This `sort` member template allows its user to pass a function pointer or function object that will be used to compare elements in the list (see *STL Function Objects* [20, 71]).

```
data.sort( std::less<float>() ); // sort ascending
data.sort( std::greater<float>() ); // sort descending
```

Here, we've instantiated two different versions of the `sort` member using the standard function object types `less` and `greater`.

Item 51 Disambiguating with Template

In *Disambiguating with Typename* [49, 169], we saw how it is sometimes necessary to tell the compiler explicitly that a nested name is a type name so that the compiler can perform a correct parse. The same situation arises with nested template names.

The canonical example is in the implementation of an STL allocator. If you're not familiar with STL allocators, don't worry, be happy. Previous familiarity with them is not necessary for following this discussion, though a good deal of patience might be.

An allocator is a class type that is used to customize memory management operations for STL containers. Allocators are typically implemented as class templates:

```
template <class T>
class AnAlloc {
  public:
    //...
    template <class Other>
    class rebind {
      public:
        typedef AnAlloc<Other> other;
    };

    //...
};
```

The class template `AnAlloc` contains the nested name `rebind`, which is itself a class template. It is used within the STL framework to create allocators "just like" the allocator that was used to instantiate a container but for a different element type. For example:

```
typedef AnAlloc<int> AI; // original allocator allocates ints
typedef AI::rebind<double>::other AD; // allocates doubles
typedef AnAlloc<double> AD; // legal! this is the same type
```

It may look a little odd, but using the `rebind` mechanism allows one to create a version of an existing allocator for a different element type without knowing the type of the allocator or the type of the element.

```
typedef SomeAlloc::rebind<Node>::other NodeAlloc;
```

If the type name `SomeAlloc` follows the STL convention for allocators, then it will have a nested `rebind` class template. Essentially, we've said, "I don't know what kind of allocator this type is, and I don't know what it allocates, but I want an allocator just like it that allocates `Node`s!"

This level of ignorance can occur only within a template, where precise types and values are not known until much later, when the template is instantiated. Consider an augmentation of our `SList` container of *Member Templates* [50, 173] to include an allocator type (`A`) that can allocate elements (of type `T`). Like the standard containers, `SList` will provide a default allocator argument:

```
template < typename T, class A = std::allocator<T> >
class SList {
    //...
    struct Node {
        //...
    };
    typedef A::rebind<Node>::other NodeAlloc; // syntax error!
    //...
};
```

As is typical for lists and other node-based containers, our list-of-`T` does not actually allocate and manipulate `T`s. Rather, it allocates and manipulates nodes that contain a member of type `T`. This is the situation we described above. We have some sort of allocator that knows how to allocate objects of type `T`, but we want to allocate objects of type `Node`. However, when we attempt to `rebind`, we get a syntax error.

Once again, the problem is that the compiler has no information about the type name `A` at this point other than that it is a type name. The compiler has to make the assumption that the nested name `rebind` is a nontemplate name, and the angle bracket that follows is parsed as a less-than. But our troubles are just beginning. Even if the compiler were somehow able to determine that `rebind` is a template name, when it reached the (doubly) nested name `other`, it would have to assume that it's a nontype name! Time for some clarification. The typedef must be written as follows:

```
typedef typename A::template rebind<Node>::other NodeAlloc;
```

The use of `template` tells the compiler that `rebind` is a template name, and the use of `typename` tells the compiler that the whole mess refers to a type name. Simple, right?

Item 52 Specializing for Type Information

Class template explicit specialization and partial specialization are commonly used to produce versions of a primary class template that are customized to specific template arguments or classes of template arguments (see *Class Template Explicit Specialization* [46, 155] and *Template Partial Specialization* [47, 161]).

However, these language features are also commonly used in an inverse fashion: Rather than produce a specialization based on the properties of a type, the properties of a type are deduced from a specialization. Let's look at a simple example:

```
template <typename T>
struct IsInt // T is not an int...
    { enum { result = false }; };
template <>
struct IsInt<int> // unless it's an int!
    { enum { result = true }; };
```

Before we go on, I'd like to point out how simple the above code is, once you get past its convoluted syntax. This is a simple example of what's known as template metaprogramming, that is, performing some portion of a computation at compile time rather than runtime through the use of template instantiation. It sounds high falutin', but it still boils down to an observation that might have come from one of my plainspoken, cranberry-farming neighbors: "It's an `int` if it's an `int`." Most advanced C++ template programming is no more difficult than this, just more involved.

With the primary template and complete specialization above, we can ask (at compile time) whether an unknown type is actually an `int`:

```
template <typename X>
void aFunc( X &arg ) {
    //...
```

```
    ...IsInt<X>::result...
    //...
}
```

The ability to ask such questions about types at compile time is the basis of a number of important optimization and error-checking techniques. Of course, knowing whether a particular type is precisely an `int` is of limited utility. Knowing whether a type is a pointer is probably more generally useful, since implementations often take different forms depending on whether they are dealing with pointers to objects or with objects directly:

```
struct Yes {}; // a type analog to true
struct No {}; // a type analog to false

template <typename T>
struct IsPtr // T is not a ptr...
    { enum { result = false }; typedef No Result; };
template <typename T>
struct IsPtr<T *> // unless it's an unqualified ptr,
    { enum { result = true }; typedef Yes Result; };
template <typename T>
struct IsPtr<T *const> // or a const ptr,
    { enum { result = true }; typedef Yes Result; };
template <typename T>
struct IsPtr<T *volatile> // or a volatile ptr,
    { enum { result = true }; typedef Yes Result; };
template <typename T>
struct IsPtr<T *const volatile> // or a const volatile ptr.
    { enum { result = true }; typedef Yes Result; };
```

We're asking a more general question with `IsPtr` than we did with `IsInt`, so we're employing partial specialization to "capture" the variously qualified versions of the pointer modifier. As advertised above, this `IsPtr` facility is really no more difficult to understand than the `IsInt` facility; it's just more syntactically challenging. (See also *SFINAE* [59, 217] for a similar metaprogramming technique.)

To see the utility of the ability to ask questions about a type at compile time, consider this implementation of a simple stack template:

```
template <typename T>
class Stack {
  public:
    ~Stack();
    void push( const T &val );
    T &top();
    void pop();
    bool empty() const;
  private:
    //...
    typedef std::deque<T> C;
    typedef typename C::iterator I;
    C s_;
};
```

Our stack is simply a pleasant interface wrapped around a standard `deque`, similar to what we could have achieved with a standard `stack` container adapter. Most of the operations are straightforward and can be implemented directly with the `deque`.

```
template <typename T>
void Stack<T>::push( const T &val )
    { s_.push_back( val ); }
```

However, we may have a problem with the `Stack`'s destructor. When the `Stack` is destroyed, its `deque` data member will be destroyed as well, which in turn will destroy any elements left in the `deque`. If these elements are pointers, however, the objects to which they point will not be deleted; that's just the way the standard `deque` container behaves. Therefore, we have to decide on a pointer element deletion policy for our `Stack`, which I will imperiously declare is to delete! (But see *Policies* [56, 205] for a more flexible approach.) We can't simply have the destructor delete the `deque` elements, however, because that would cause an error in those cases where the elements are not pointers.

One solution would be to use partial specialization of the `Stack` (primary) template to handle stacks of pointers (see *Template Partial Specialization*

[47, 161]). However, that seems like an overreaction when only a small portion of the Stack's behavior must change. A different approach simply asks the obvious question (at compile time) and acts accordingly: "If the element type of the Stack is a pointer, then delete any remaining elements. Otherwise don't delete."

```
template <typename T>
class Stack {
  public:
    ~Stack()
        { cleanup( typename IsPtr<T>::Result() ); }
    //...
  private:
    void cleanup( Yes ) {
        for( I i( s_.begin() ); i != s_.end(); ++i )
            delete *i;
    }
    void cleanup( No )
        {}
    typedef std::deque<T> C;
    typedef typename C::iterator I;
    C s_;
};
```

Here we have two different cleanup member functions, one of which takes an argument of type Yes, while the other takes an argument of type No. The Yes version deletes; the No version does not. The destructor asks the question "Is T a pointer type?" by instantiating IsPtr with T and accessing the nested type name Result (see *Disambiguating with Typename* [49, 169]), which will be either Yes or No, and passing an object of that type to cleanup. Only one of the two versions of cleanup will be instantiated and called, and the other will not (see *You Instantiate What You Use* [61, 225]).

```
Stack<Shape *> shapes; // will delete
Stack<std::string> names; // won't delete
```

Class template specializations can be used to extract arbitrarily complex information from types. For instance, we may want to know not only whether a particular type is an array but, if it is an array, what it's an array of and what its bound is:

```
template <typename T>
struct IsArray { // T is not an array...
    enum { result = false };
    typedef No Result;
};
template <typename E, int b>
struct IsArray<E [b]> { // ...unless it's an array!
    enum { result = true };
    typedef Yes Result;
    enum { bound = b }; // array bound
    typedef E Etype; // array element type
};
```

We may want to know not only whether a particular type is a pointer to data member, but, if it is, what its class and member types are:

```
template <typename T>
struct IsPCM { // T is not a pointer to data member
    enum { result = false };
    typedef No Result;
};
template <class C, typename T>
struct IsPCM<T C::*> { // ...unless it is!
    enum { result = true };
    typedef Yes Result;
    typedef C ClassType; // the class type
    typedef T MemberType; // the type of class member
};
```

These techniques are employed in a number of popular toolkits that provide the ability to access type traits (see *Traits* [54, 193]) for compile-time code customization.

Item 53 | Embedded Type Information

How do we know the type of a container's elements?

```
template <typename T>
class Seq {
    //...
};
```

At first, this may not seem to be a problem. The element type of `Seq<std::string>` is `std::string`, right? Not necessarily. There's nothing to prevent the implementation of our (nonstandard) sequence container from making the element type `const T`, `T *`, or a "smart pointer" to a `T`. (A particularly weird container could simply ignore the template parameter and always set the element type to `void *`!) But vagary of implementation is not the only reason we may not be able to determine the element type of our container. We often write generic code in which that information is simply not available.

```
template <class Container>
Elem process( Container &c, int size ) {
    Temp temp = Elem();
    for( int i = 0; i < size; ++i )
        temp += c[i];
    return temp;
}
```

In the `process` generic algorithm above, we need to know the element type (`Elem`) of `Container`, as well as a type that could serve to declare a temporary for holding objects of the element type (`Temp`), but that information is not available until the `process` function template is instantiated with a specific container.

A common way to handle this situation is to have a type provide "personal" information about itself. This information is often embedded in the type itself, rather like embedding a microchip in a person that can be queried for the person's name, identifying number, blood type, and so on.

(This is an analogy, not an indication of approval for employment of such a procedure.) We are not interested in our sequence container's blood type, but we do want to know the type of its elements.

```
template <class T>
class Seq {
  public:
    typedef T Elem; // element type
    typedef T Temp; // temporary type
    size_t size() const;
    //...
};
```

This embedded information can be queried at compile time:

```
typedef Seq<std::string> Strings;
//...
Strings::Elem aString;
```

This approach is familiar to any user of the standard library containers. For instance, to declare an iterator into a standard container, it's advisable to ask the container itself what its iterator type is:

```
vector<int> aVec;
//...
for( vector<int>::iterator i( aVec.begin() );
    i != aVec.end(); ++i )
    //...
```

Here we've asked the `vector<int>` to tell us what its iterator type is, rather than make the assumption that it is `int *` (as it often is for many implementations). The iterator type for `vector<int>` could just as well be some other type (like a user-defined safe pointer type), so the only portable way to write the loop above is to get the type of the iterator from the `vector<int>` itself.

A more important observation is that this approach allows us to write generic code that makes the *assumption* that the required information is present.

```
template <class Container>
typename Container::Elem process( Container &c, int size ) {
```

```
    typename Container::Temp temp
        = typename Container::Elem();
    for( int i = 0; i < size; ++i )
        temp += c[i];
    return temp;
}
```

This version of the `process` algorithm queries the `Container` type for its personal information, and makes the assumption that `Container` defines the nested type names `Elem` and `Temp`. (Note that we had to use the `typename` keyword in three places to tell the compiler explicitly that the nested names were type names and not some other kind of nested name. See *Disambiguating with Typename* [49, 169].)

```
Strings strings;
aString = process( strings, strings.size() ); // OK
```

The `process` algorithm works well with our `Seq` container and will also work with any other container that follows our convention.

```
template <typename T>
class ReadonlySeq {
  public:
    typedef const T Elem;
    typedef T Temp;
    //...
};
```

We can `process` a `ReadonlySeq` container because it validates our assumptions.

Item 54 | Traits

Sometimes it's not enough to know just an object's type. Often, there is information related to the object's type that is essential to working with the object. In *Embedded Type Information* [53, 189], we saw how complex types like the standard containers often embed information about themselves within themselves:

```
Strings strings;
aString = process( strings, strings.size() );  // OK
std::vector<std::string> strings2;
aString = process( strings2, strings2.size() ); // error!
extern double readings[RSIZ];
double r = process( readings, RSIZ ); // error!
```

The `process` algorithm works well with our `Seq` container but fails with a standard `vector` container, because `vector` does not define the nested type names that `process` assumes are present.

We can `process` a `ReadonlySeq` container because it validates our assumptions, but we may also want to `process` containers that do not follow our rather parochial convention, and we may want to `process` container-like things that are not even classes. Traits classes are often used to solve these problems.

A traits class is a collection of information about a type. Unlike our nested container information, however, the traits class is independent of the type it describes.

```
template <typename Cont>
struct ContainerTraits;
```

One common use of a traits class is to put a conventional layer between our generic algorithms and types that don't follow the algorithms' expected convention. We write the algorithm in terms of the type's traits. The general case will often assume some sort of convention. In this case, our `ContainerTraits` will assume the convention used by our `Seq` and `ReadonlySeq` containers.

```
template <typename Cont>
struct ContainerTraits {
    typedef typename Cont::Elem Elem;
    typedef typename Cont::Temp Temp;
    typedef typename Cont::Ptr Ptr;
};
```

With the addition of this traits class template, we have the choice of referring to the nested `Elem` type of one of our container types either through the container type or through the traits type instantiated with the container type.

```
typedef Seq<int> Cont;
Cont::Elem e1;
ContainerTraits<Cont>::Elem e2; // same type as e1
```

We can rewrite our generic algorithm to employ traits in place of direct access to the container's nested type names:

```
template <typename Container>
typename ContainerTraits<Container>::Elem
process( Container &c, int size ) {
    typename ContainerTraits<Container>::Temp temp
        = typename ContainerTraits<Container>::Elem();
    for( int i = 0; i < size; ++i )
        temp += c[i];
    return temp;
}
```

It may seem that all we've managed to do is to make the syntax of the generic `process` algorithm even more impenetrable! Previously, to get the type of the container's element, we wrote `typename Container::Elem`. Put in plain language, we said, "Get `Container`'s nested name `Elem`. By the way, it's a type name." With traits, we have to write `typename ContainerTraits<Container>::Elem`. Essentially, we say, "Instantiate the `ContainerTraits` class that corresponds to this container, and get its nested name `Elem`. By the way, it's a type name." We've taken a step back from getting the information directly from the container type itself and are going through the intermediary of the traits class. If accessing nested type information is like reading information about a person from an embedded microchip, using a traits class is like looking up someone's information in a database, using the person's name as a key. You'll get the same information, but the database lookup approach is certainly less invasive and more flexible.

For example, you can't get information from someone's microchip if he doesn't have one. (Perhaps the person comes from a region where embedded microchips are not *de rigeur*.) However, you can always create a new entry in a database for such a person without the necessity of even informing the individual concerned. Similarly, we can specialize the traits template to provide information about a particular nonconforming container without affecting the container itself:

```
class ForeignContainer {
    // no nested type information...
};
//...
template <>
struct ContainerTraits<ForeignContainer> {
    typedef int Elem;
    typedef Elem Temp;
    typedef Elem *Ptr;
};
```

With this specialization of `ContainerTraits` available, we can `process` a `ForeignContainer` as effectively as one that is written to our convention. The original implementation of `process` would have failed on a `ForeignContainer` because it would have attempted to access nested information that did not exist:

```
ForeignContainer::Elem x; // error, no such nested name!
ContainerTraits<ForeignContainer>::Elem y; // OK, using traits
```

It's helpful to think of a traits template as a collection of information that is indexed by a type, much as an associative container is indexed by a key. But the "indexing" of traits happens at compile time, through template specialization.

Another advantage of accessing information about a type through a traits class is that the technique can be used to provide information about types that are not classes and therefore can have no nested information. Even though traits classes are classes, the types whose traits they encapsulate don't have to be. For example, an array is a kind of (mathematically and morally) degenerate container that we might like to manipulate as a first class container.

```
template <>
struct ContainerTraits<const char *> {
    typedef const char Elem;
    typedef char Temp;
    typedef const char *Ptr;
};
```

With this specialization in place for the "container" type `const char *`, we can `process` an array of characters.

```
const char *name = "Arsene Lupin";
const char *r = process( name, strlen(name) );
```

We can continue in this fashion for other types of arrays, producing specializations for `int *`, `const double *`, and so on. However, it would be more convenient to specify a single case for any type of pointer, since they all will have similar properties. For this purpose, we employ partial specialization of the traits template for pointers:

```
template <typename T>
struct ContainerTraits<T *> {
    typedef T Elem;
    typedef T Temp;
    typedef T *Ptr;
};
```

Specializing `ContainerTraits` with any pointer type, whether it be `int *` or `const float *(*const*)(int)`, will result in instantiation of this partial specialization, unless there is an even more specialized version of `ContainerTraits` available.

```
extern double readings[RSIZ];
double r = process( readings, RSIZ ); // works!
```

We're not quite there yet, however. Notice that using the partial specialization for a pointer to constant will not result in the correct type for use as a "temporary." That is, constant temporary values are not of much use because we can't assign to them. What we'd like is to have the non-constant analog of the element type as our temporary type. In the case of `const char *`, for instance, `ContainerTraits<const char *>::Temp` should be `char`, not `const char`. We can handle this case with an additional partial specialization:

```
template <typename T>
struct ContainerTraits<const T *> {
    typedef const T Elem;
    typedef T Temp; // note: non-const analog of Elem
    typedef const T *Ptr;
};
```

This more specific partial specialization will be selected in preference to the previous one in those cases where the template argument is a pointer to constant, rather than a pointer to non-constant.

Partial specialization can also help us to extend our traits mechanism to convert a "foreign" convention to be in line with a local convention. For example, the STL is very heavy on convention (see *The Standard Template Library* [4, 11]), and the standard containers have concepts similar to those encapsulated in our `ContainerTraits` but are expressed differently. For example, we earlier attempted to instantiate the `process` algorithm with a standard `vector` but failed. Let's fix that.

```
template <class T>
struct ContainerTraits< std::vector<T> > {
    typedef typename std::vector<T>::value_type Elem;
    typedef typename
        std::iterator_traits<typename
        std::vector<T>::iterator>
        ::value_type Temp;
    typedef typename
        std::iterator_traits<typename
        std::vector<T>::iterator>
        ::pointer Ptr;
};
```

It's not the most readable implementation one can imagine, but it's hidden, and our users can now invoke our generic algorithm with a container generated from a standard `vector`.

```
std::vector<std::string> strings2;
aString = process( strings2, strings2.size() ); // works!
```

Item 55 Template Template Parameters

Let's pick up the `Stack` template we considered in *Specializing for Type Information* [52, 183]. We decided to implement it with a standard `deque`, which is a pretty good compromise choice of implementation, though in many circumstances a different container would be more efficient or appropriate. We can address this problem by adding an additional template parameter to `Stack` for the container type used in its implementation.

```
template <typename T, class Cont>
class Stack;
```

For simplicity, let's abandon the standard library (not usually a good idea, by the way) and assume we have available a set of nonstandard container templates: `List`, `Vector`, `Deque`, and perhaps others. Let's also assume these containers are similar to the standard containers but have only a single template parameter for the element type of the container.

Recall that the standard containers actually have at least two parameters: the element type and an allocator type. Containers use allocators to allocate and free their working memory so that this behavior may be customized. In effect, the allocator specifies a memory management policy for the container (see *Policies* [56, 205]). The allocator has a default so it's easy to forget it's there. However, when you instantiate a standard container like `vector<int>`, you're actually getting `vector< int, std::allocator<int> >`.

For example, the declaration of our nonstandard `List` would be

```
template <typename> class List;
```

Notice that we've left out the name of template parameter in the declaration of `List`, above. Just as with a formal argument name in a function declaration, giving a name to a template parameter in a template declaration is optional. As with a function definition, the name of a template parameter is required only in a template definition and only if the parameter name is used in the template. However, as with formal arguments in function declarations, it's common to give names to template parameters in template declarations to help document the template.

```
template <typename T, class Cont>
class Stack {
  public:
    ~Stack();
    void push( const T & );
    //...
  private:
    Cont s_;
};
```

A user of `Stack` now has to provide two template arguments, an element type and a container type, and the container has to be able to hold objects of the element type.

```
Stack<int, List<int> > aStack1; // OK
Stack<double, List<int> > aStack2; // legal, not OK
Stack<std::string, Deque<char *> > aStack3; // error!
```

The declarations of `aStack2` and `aStack3` show we have a potential problem in coordination. If the user selects the incorrect type of container for the element type, we'll get a compile-time error (in the case of `aStack3`, because of the inability to copy a `string` to a `char *`) or a subtle bug (in the case of `aStack2`, because of loss of precision in copying a `double` to an `int`). Additionally, most users of `Stack` don't want to be bothered with selection of its underlying implementation and will be satisfied with a reasonable default. We can improve the situation by providing a default for the second template parameter.

```
template <typename T, class Cont = Deque<T> >
class Stack {
    //...
};
```

This helps in cases where the user of a `Stack` is willing to accept a `Deque` implementation or doesn't particularly care about the implementation.

```
Stack<int> aStack1; // container is Deque<int>
Stack<double> aStack2; // container is Deque<double>
```

This is more or less the approach employed by the standard container adapters `stack`, `queue`, and `priority_queue`.

```
std::stack<int> stds; // container is
                      // deque< int, allocator<int> >
```

This approach is a good compromise of convenience for the casual user of the `Stack` facility and of flexibility for the experienced user to employ any (legal and effective) kind of container to hold the `Stack`'s elements.

However, this flexibility comes at a cost in safety. It's still necessary to coordinate the types of element and container in other specializations, and this requirement of coordination opens up the possibility of miscoordination.

```
Stack<int, List<int> > aStack3;
Stack<int, List<unsigned> > aStack4; // oops!
```

Let's see if we can improve safety and still have reasonable flexibility. A template can take a parameter that is itself the name of a template. These parameters have the pleasingly repetitious name of template template parameters.

```
template <typename T, template <typename> class Cont>
class Stack;
```

This new template parameter list for `Stack` looks unnerving, but it's not as bad as it appears. The first parameter, `T`, is old hat. It's just the name of a type. The second parameter, `Cont`, is a template template parameter. It's the name of a class template that has a single type name parameter. Note that we didn't give a name to the type name parameter of `Cont`, although we could have:

```
template <typename T, template <typename ElementType> class Cont>
class Stack;
```

However, such a name (`ElementType`, above) can serve only as documentation, similar to a formal argument name in a function declaration. These names are commonly omitted, but you should feel free to use them where you think they improve readability. Conversely, we could take the opportunity to reduce readability to a minimum by eliminating all technically unnecessary names in the declaration of `Stack`:

```
template <typename, template <typename> class>
class Stack;
```

But compassion for the readers of our code does impose constraints on such practices, even if the C++ language does not.

The `Stack` template uses its type name parameter to instantiate its template template parameter. The resulting container type is used to implement the `Stack`:

```
template <typename T, template <typename> class Cont>
class Stack {
    //...
  private:
    Cont<T> s_;
};
```

This approach allows coordination between element and container to be handled by the implementation of the `Stack` itself, rather than in all the various code that specializes `Stack`. This single point of specialization reduces the possibility of miscoordination between the element type and the container used to hold the elements.

```
Stack<int,List> aStack1;
Stack<std::string,Deque> aStack2;
```

For additional convenience, we can employ a default for the template template argument:

```
template <typename T, template <typename> class Cont = Deque>
class Stack {
    //...
};
//...
Stack<int> aStack1; // use default: Cont is Deque
Stack<std::string,List> aStack2; // Cont is List
```

This is often a good approach for dealing with coordination of a set of arguments to a template and a template that is to be instantiated with the arguments.

It's common to confuse template template parameters with type name parameters that just happen to be generated from templates. For example, consider the following class template declaration:

```
template <class Cont> class Wrapper1;
```

The `Wrapper1` template needs a type name for its template argument. (We used the keyword `class` instead of `typename` in the declaration of the `Cont` parameter of `Wrapper1` to tell the readers of our code that we're expecting a `class` or `struct` rather than an arbitrary type, but it's all the same to the compiler. In this context `typename` and `class` mean exactly the same thing technically. See *Optional Keywords* [63, 231].) That type name could be generated from a template, as in `Wrapper1< List<int> >`, but `List<int>` is still just a class name, even though it was generated from a template.

```
Wrapper1< List<int> > w1; // fine, List<int> is a type name
Wrapper1< std::list<int> > w2; // fine, list<int> is a type
Wrapper1<List> w3; // error! List is a template name
```

Alternatively, consider the following class template declaration:

```
template <template <typename> class Cont> class Wrapper2;
```

The `Wrapper2` template needs a template name for its template argument, and not just any template name. The declaration says that the template must take a single type argument.

```
Wrapper2<List> w4; // fine, List is a template one type
Wrapper2< List<int> > w5; // error! List<int> isn't a template
Wrapper2<std::list> w6; // error! std::list takes 2+ arguments
```

If we want to have a chance at being able to specialize with a standard container, we have to do the following:

```
template <template <typename Element,
    class Allocator> class Cont>
class Wrapper3;
```

or equivalently:

```
template <template <typename,typename> class Cont>
class Wrapper3;
```

This declaration says that the template must take two type name arguments:

```
Wrapper3<std::list> w7; // might work...
Wrapper3< std::list<int> > w8; // error! list<int> is a class
Wrapper3<List> w9; // error! List takes one type argument
```

However, the standard container templates (like `list`) may legally be declared to take more than two parameters, so the declaration of `w7` above may not work on all platforms. Well, we all love and respect the STL, but we never claimed it was perfect.

Item 56 | Policies

In *Specializing for Type Information* [52, 183], we designed a stack template that deleted any remaining elements left in the stack at the end of the stack's lifetime if the stack's element type was a pointer.

```
template <typename T> class Stack;
```

This is not an unreasonable policy, but it is inflexible. There may be cases where the user of our stack does not want to delete what the stack's pointers refer to. For instance, the pointers may refer to objects that are not on the heap or that are shared with other containers. Additionally, it's possible that a pointer refers to an array of objects, rather than a single object. If we have a stack of character pointers, this is almost certainly the case, since character pointers usually refer to an NTCTS (standardese for a null terminated array of characters):

```
Stack<const char *> names; // oops!  undefined behavior
```

Our deletion policy assumes that a `Stack`'s pointers refer to a single object, and therefore employs the nonarray form of `delete`, whereas for an array we must use array delete (see *Array Allocation* [37, 127]).

Our goal is to be able to write the `Stack` template's destructor in something like the following way:

```
template <typename T>
class Stack {
  public:
    ~Stack() {
        for( I i( s_.begin() ); i != s_.end(); ++i )
            doDeletionPolicy( *i );
    }
    //...
  private:
    typedef std::deque<T> C;
    typedef typename C::iterator I;
```

```
    C s_;
};
```

The destructor iterates over any remaining elements and executes the appropriate deletion policy on each element. The doDeletionPolicy could be implemented in a variety of ways. Typically, a policy is made explicit when the Stack template is instantiated and is implemented with a template template parameter (see *Template Template Parameters* [55, 199]).

```
template <typename T, template <typename> class DeletionPolicy>
class Stack {
  public:
    ~Stack() {
        for( I i( s_.begin() ); i != s_.end(); ++i )
            DeletionPolicy<T>::doDelete( *i ); // exec policy
    }
    //...
  private:
    typedef std::deque<T> C;
    typedef typename C::iterator I;
    C s_;
};
```

By examining how the deletion policy is used in the Stack destructor, we can determine that a Stack's deletion policy is a class template that is instantiated with the element type of the Stack. It has a static member function called doDelete that performs the appropriate deletion action on the Stack element. Now we can go about defining some appropriate policies. One policy is to delete:

```
template <typename T>
struct PtrDeletePolicy {
    static void doDelete( T ptr )
        { delete ptr; }
};
```

Of course, we could have designed a policy implementation with a different interface. For example, rather than use a static member function, we could have overloaded the function call operator

```
template <typename T>
struct PtrDeletePolicy {
```

```
    void operator ()( T ptr )
        { delete ptr; }
};
```

and modified the deletion operation in Stack's destructor to read

```
DeletionPolicy<T>()(*i);
```

The important thing is to establish a convention, because every implementation of a particular policy will be accessed with the same syntax.

Other useful policies perform an array deletion or do nothing at all:

```
template <typename T>
struct ArrayDeletePolicy {
    static void doDelete( T ptr )
        { delete [] ptr; }
};
template <typename T>
struct NoDeletePolicy {
    static void doDelete( const T & )
        {}
};
```

Now we can specify the appropriate deletion policy when we instantiate `Stack`:

```
Stack<int, NoDeletePolicy> s1; // don't delete ints
Stack<std::string *, PtrDeletePolicy> s2; // delete string *'s
Stack<const char *, ArrayDeletePolicy> s3; // delete [] these
Stack<const char *, NoDeletePolicy> s4; // don't delete!
Stack<int, PtrDeletePolicy> s5; // error! can't delete int!
```

If one policy is more commonly used than others, it's often a good idea to make it the default:

```
template <typename T,
    template <typename> class DeletionPolicy = NoDeletePolicy>
class Stack;
//...
Stack<int> s6; // don't delete
```

```
Stack<const char *> s7; // don't delete
Stack<const char *, ArrayDeletePolicy> s8; // delete []
```

A template design often offers several opportunities for parameterization by policies. For example, in *Template Template Parameters* [55, 199] we gave the user the ability to specify how a `Stack` was implemented. That's an implementation policy:

```
template <typename T,
    template <typename> class DeletionPolicy = NoDeletePolicy
    template <typename> class Cont = Deque>
class Stack;
```

This gives the user of `Stack` additional flexibility:

```
Stack<double *, ArrayDeletePolicy, Vector> dailyReadings;
```

while allowing good general behavior in the default case.

```
Stack<double> moreReadings; // no deletion, use a Deque
```

In generic design, we frequently make policy decisions about implementation and behavior. Often, those decisions can be abstracted and represented as policies.

Item 57 Template Argument Deduction

Class templates must be specialized explicitly. For example, if we want to specialize the `Heap` container discussed in *Class Template Explicit Specialization* [46, 155], we have to provide a type name argument to the template:

```
Heap<int> aHeap;
Heap<const char *> anotherHeap;
```

Function templates may also be specialized explicitly. Suppose we have a function template that performs a restricted old-style cast:

```
template <typename R, typename E>
R cast( const E &expr ) {
    // ...do some clever checking...
    return R( expr ); // ...and cast.
}
```

We may specialize the template explicitly when we call it, just as we must specialize a class template:

```
int a = cast<int,double>(12.3);
```

However, it's typical and more convenient to let the compiler deduce the template arguments from the types of the actual arguments to the function call. Not surprisingly, this process is called "template argument deduction." Careful! In the description below, pay attention to the difference between the terms "template argument" and "function argument" (see *Template Terminology* [45, 153]). Consider a template with a single template argument that finds the lesser of two function arguments.

```
template <typename T>
T min( const T &a, const T &b )
    { return a < b ? a : b; }
```

When we use `min` without supplying the template arguments explicitly, the compiler examines the types of the function call arguments in order to deduce the template argument:

```
int a = min( 12, 13 ); // T is int
double d = min( '\b', '\a' ); // T is char
char c = min( 12.3, 4 ); // error! T can't be both double and int
```

The erroneous line above is the result of the compiler's not being able to deduce a template argument in an ambiguous situation. In such cases, we can always tell the compiler what a template argument is by being explicit:

```
d = min<double>( 12.3, 4 ); // OK, T is double
```

A similar situation occurs with our `cast` template if we try to use template argument deduction:

```
int a = cast( 12.3 ); // error! E is double, but what's R?
```

As with overload resolution, the compiler examines the types of only function arguments during template argument deduction, not potential return types. The only way the compiler's going to know the return type is if we tell it:

```
int a = cast<int>( 12.3 ); // E is double and
                           // R is (explicitly) int
```

Notice that any trailing template arguments may be left off the template argument list if the compiler can deduce them on its own. In this case we had only to supply the compiler with the return type and let it figure out the expression type on its own. The order of the template parameters is important for the template's usability, since if the expression type had preceded the return type, we would have had to specify both explicitly.

At this point, many people will notice the syntax of the call to `cast` above and ask, "Are you implying that `static_cast`, `dynamic_cast`, `const_cast`, and `reinterpret_cast` are function templates?" No, we're not implying that because these four cast operators are not templates, they're built-in operators (like the `new` operator or the `+` operator on integers); but it sure looks like their syntax was inspired by something similar to our `cast` function template. (See *New Cast Operators* [9, 29].)

Note that template argument deduction works by examining the types of the actual arguments to a call. This implies that any template argument of a function template that cannot be deduced from the argument types has to be supplied explicitly. For example, here's an annoyingly repetitious function template:

```
template <int n, typename T>
void repeat( const T &msg ) {
    for( int i = 0; i < n; ++i )
        std::cout << msg << std::flush;
}
```

We were careful to put the integer template argument before the type argument, so we could get by with specifying only the number of repetitions of the message, and let template argument deduction determine the type of the message:

```
repeat<12>( 42 ); // n is 12, T is int
repeat<MAXINT>( '\a' ); // n is big, T is char
```

In the `cast`, `min`, and `repeat` templates, the compiler deduced a single template argument from a single function argument. However, the deduction mechanism is capable of deducing multiple template arguments from the type of a single function argument:

```
template <int bound, typename T>
void zeroOut( T (&ary)[bound] ) {
    for( int i = 0; i < bound; ++i )
        ary[i] = T();
}
//...
const int hrsinweek = 7*24;
float readings[hrsinweek];
zeroOut( readings ); // bound == 168, T is float
```

In this case, `zeroOut` expects an array argument, and argument deduction is capable of dissecting the argument type to determine its bound and element type.

We noted at the start of this item that a class template must be specialized explicitly. However, function template argument deduction can be used to specialize a class template indirectly. Consider a class template that can be used to generate a function object from a function pointer (see *STL Function Objects* [20, 71]):

```
template <typename A1, typename A2, typename R>
class PFun2 : public std::binary_function<A1,A2,R> {
  public:
    explicit PFun2( R (*fp)(A1,A2) ) : fp_( fp ) {}
    R operator()( A1 a1, A2 a2 ) const
        { return fp_( a1, a2 ); }
  private:
    R (*fp_)(A1,A2);
};
```

(This is a simplified version of the standard `pointer_to_binary_function` template and has been chosen specifically for the convoluted syntax required to specialize it. It doesn't get much worse than this.) Instantiating the template directly is somewhat onerous:

```
bool isGreater( int, int );
std::sort(b, e, PFun2<int,int,bool>(isGreater)); // painful
```

It's common in cases like this to provide a "helper function" whose only purpose is to deduce the template arguments in order to specialize, automagically, a class template:

```
template <typename R, typename A1, typename A2>
inline PFun2<A1,A2,R> makePFun( R (*pf)(A1,A2) )
    { return PFun2<A1,A2,R>(pf); }
//...
std::sort(b, e, makePFun(isGreater)); // much better...
```

In this deduction tour de force, the compiler is able to deduce both argument types and the return type from the type of a single function argument. This technique is commonly used in the standard library for utilities like `ptr_fun`, `make_pair`, `mem_fun`, `back_inserter`, and many others that are simply helper functions that ease the task of complex and error-prone class template specialization.

Item 58 | Overloading Function Templates

Function templates can be overloaded with other function templates and with nontemplate functions. This capability is useful but easy to abuse.

One of the major differences between function templates and nontemplate functions is the availability of implicit conversions of actual arguments. Nontemplate functions allow a wide range of implicit conversions on their arguments, from built-in conversions (like integral promotions) to user-defined conversions (nonexplicit single argument constructors and conversion operators). In the case of function templates, because the compiler must perform argument deduction based on the types of the arguments, only trivial implicit conversions will be performed, including outer-level qualification (for example, `T` to `const T` or `const T` to `T`), reference (for example, `T` to `T &`), and array and function decay to a pointer (for example, `T[42]` to `T *`).

The practical effect of this difference is that function templates require much more exact matching than nontemplate functions do. This can be good, bad, or merely surprising. For example, consider the following:

```
template <typename T>
void g( T a, T b ) { ... } // this g is a template
void g( char a, char b ) { ... } // this g is not
//...
g( 12.3, 45.6 ); // template g
g( 12.3, 45 ); // non-template g!
```

The first call with two `double` arguments could be made to match the nontemplate `g` by converting the `doubles` to `char` implicitly (legal but inadvisable), but an exact match is available by instantiating the template `g` with `T` as `double`, so the template is chosen. The second call with `double` and `int` arguments will not match the template `g`, because the compiler will not attempt the predefined conversion from `int` to `double` on the second argument (or from `double` to `int` on the first) so as to deduce `T` to be `double` (or `int`). Therefore the non-member `g` is called, using the unfortunate predefined conversions of `double` and `int` to `char`.

Selecting the right version of a function when faced with a variety of template and nontemplate candidates is a complex process, and many otherwise reliable C++ compilers will select the incorrect function or issue an inappropriate error. This is also an indication that the maintainers of our code may have similar difficulties in understanding what version of an overloaded template we intended to call. For everybody's sake, when using function template overloading, keep things as simple as possible.

"Simple" doesn't imply unsophisticated. In *Template Argument Deduction* [57, 209], we considered a "helper" function that was used to circumvent an onerous and error-prone specialization of a complex class template:

```
template <typename A1, typename A2, typename R>
class PFun2 : public std::binary_function<A1,A2,R> {
    // see implementation in Template Argument
    // Deduction [57, 209] ...
};
```

Rather than force users to specialize this monster directly, we provided a helper function that performed template argument deduction and specialization:

```
template <typename R, typename A1, typename A2>
inline PFun2<A1,A2,R> makePFun( R (*pf)(A1,A2) )
    { return PFun2<A1,A2,R>(pf); }
```

Syntactically, this is a fairly complex piece of code, but it simplifies things for our users, allowing them to write `makePFun(isGreater)` rather than `PFun2<int,int,bool>(isGreater)` for a function declared `bool isGreater(int,int)`.

Of course, we'll want to provide facilities for unary functions as well:

```
template <typename A, typename R>
class PFun1 : public std::unary_function<A,R> {
  public:
    explicit PFun1( R (*fp)(A) ) : fp_( fp ) {}
    R operator()( A a ) const
        { return fp_( a ); }
```

```
  private:
    R (*fp_)(A);
};
```

And a helper function:

```
template <typename R, typename A>
inline PFun1<A,R> makePFun( R (*pf)(A) )
    { return PFun1<A,R>(pf); }
```

Here is a perfect application of function template overloading. It's simple, in the sense that there is no possible confusion about which version of `makePFun` will be called (one is for binary functions, one for unary functions), but use of the same name for both functions makes the facility easy to learn and use.

Item 59 | SFINAE

In attempting to use function template argument deduction to select among a number of overloaded function templates and nontemplate functions, the compiler may attempt a specialization that fails on one or more of them.

```
template <typename T> void f( T );
template <typename T> void f( T * );
//...
f( 1024 ); // instantiates first f
```

Even though substitution of the nonzero integer for `T *` in the second `f` function template would have been incorrect, the attempted substitution does not give rise to an error provided that a correct substitution is found. In this case, the first `f` is instantiated, and there is no error. Thus, we have the "substitution failure is not an error" concept, dubbed SFINAE by Vandevoorde and Josuttis.

SFINAE is an important property in that, without it, it would be difficult to overload function templates; the combination of argument deduction and overloading would otherwise render many uses of a set of overloaded function templates illegal. But SFINAE is also valuable as a metaprogramming technique.

Recall the `IsPtr` facility we developed in *Specializing for Type Information* [52, 183]. There we used template partial specialization in order to determine whether an unknown type was a pointer of some kind. We can use SFINAE to achieve a similar result.

```
typedef True char; // sizeof(True) == 1
typedef struct { char a[2]; } False; // sizeof(False) > 1
//...
template <typename T> True isPtr( T * );
False isPtr( ... );

#define is_ptr( e ) (sizeof(isPtr(e))==sizeof(True))
```

Here, we can use `is_ptr` to determine whether the type of an expression is a pointer through a combination of function template argument deduction and SFINAE. If the expression `e` has pointer type, the compiler will match the template function `isPtr`; otherwise it will match the non-template `isPtr` function with the ellipsis formal argument. SFINAE assures us that the attempt to match the template `isPtr` with a non-pointer will not result in a compile-time error.

The second bit of magic is the use of `sizeof` in the `is_ptr` macro. Notice that neither `isPtr` function is defined. This is correct, because they are never actually called. The appearance of a function call in a `sizeof` expression causes the compiler to perform argument deduction and function matching, but it doesn't actually call the function. The `sizeof` operator is interested only in the size of the return type of the function that would have been called. We can then check the size of the function's return type to determine which function was matched. If the compiler selected the function template, then the expression `e` had pointer type.

We did not have to special case for const pointers, volatile pointers, and const volatile pointers as we did for the `IsPtr` facility that we implemented with class template partial specialization. As part of function template argument deduction, the compiler will ignore "first level" cv-qualifiers (`const` and `volatile`) as well as reference modifiers (see *Overloading Function Templates* [58, 213]). Similarly, we do not have to be concerned about incorrectly identifying as a pointer type a user-defined type that has a conversion operator to a pointer type. The compiler employs a very restricted list of conversions on the actual arguments during function template argument deduction, and user-defined conversions are not on the list.

Notice the similarity of this technique with our use of template partial specialization to uncover type information in *Specializing for Type Information* [52, 183]. There we used the primary template as a "catchall" and used complete or partial specialization to detect the cases of interest. Here, we're using a function with an ellipsis formal argument as the catchall and capturing cases of interest with more precisely overloaded versions of the catchall. In fact, class template partial specialization and function template overloading are very closely related technically; the standard actually defines the selection algorithm for one in terms of the other.

After one gets used to the `is_ptr` example above, there really is nothing more to the SFINAE technique from a technical perspective. However, this simple technique can be employed in rather surprising ways to uncover information about types and expressions at compile time. Let's look at some (not at all simple) examples.

Consider the problem of determining whether an unknown type is a class:

```
template <typename T>
struct IsClass {
    template <class C> static True isClass( int C::* );
    template <typename C> static False isClass( ... );
    enum { r = sizeof(IsClass<T>::isClass<T>(0))
        == sizeof(True) };
};
```

Neatness counts, so this time we've encapsulated the SFINAE mechanism inside a class template, `IsClass`, and overloaded two function templates as static members of `IsClass`. One of the functions takes a pointer to member argument (see *Pointers to Class Members Are Not Pointers* [15, 53]). A literal zero can be converted to a pointer to class member (even for a function template), so if `T` is a class type, the first `isClass` will be matched. If `T` is not a class, SFINAE will ignore the erroneous first matching attempt and choose the version of `isClass` with the ellipsis argument list. As with `is_ptr`, we can check the size of the function's return type to see which function was matched and, thereby, determine whether `T` is a class.

This next example is abstracted from Vandevoorde and Josuttis: Suppose you'd like to know whether a particular class type has a nested type name spelled "iterator." (Of course, this can be implemented to ask the question of any nested type name, not just `iterator`.)

```
template <class C>
True hasIterator( typename C::iterator const * );
template <typename T>
False hasIterator( ... );
#define has_iterator( C )\
    (sizeof(hasIterator<C>(0))==sizeof(True))
```

This has_iterator facility is mechanically identical to IsClass, but this time we're accessing a nested type name of an unknown type (see *Disambiguating with Typename* [49, 169]). If C has such a nested type, we'll be able to convert the literal zero to a pointer to such a type; otherwise we'll match the catchall.

Finally, let's look at some trickery from Andrei Alexandrescu: Given two unknown types T1 and T2, can we convert T1 to T2? Note that this mechanism will detect both predefined and user-defined conversions:

```
template <typename T1, typename T2>
struct CanConvert {
    static True canConvert( T2 );
    static False canConvert( ... );
    static T1 makeT1();
    enum { r = sizeof(canConvert( makeT1() )) == sizeof(True) };
};
```

As we saw in our Heap implementation in *Specializing for Type Information* [52, 183], there is often a great advantage in flexibility or efficiency in being able to provide special-purpose implementations based on information that can be statically determined at compile time. Through the use of SFINAE and other metaprogramming techniques, we're able to ask questions like, "Is this unknown type a pointer to a class type that has a nested iterator typename that can be converted to std::string?"

Item 60 | Generic Algorithms

A generic algorithm is a function template that is designed in such a way that it can be easily and effectively customized at compile time according to the context of its use. Let's look at a function template that doesn't meet these exacting standards and is therefore not a proper generic algorithm:

```
template <typename T>
void slowSort( T a[], int len ) {
    for( int i = 0; i < len; ++i ) // For each pair
        for( int j = i; j < len; ++j )
            if( a[j] < a[i] ) { // ...if out of order...
                T tmp( a[j] ); // ...swap them.
                a[j] = a[i];
                a[i] = tmp;
            }
}
```

This template can be used to sort an array of objects, provided that the objects can be compared with a < operator and copied. For example, we can sort an array of our `String` objects from *Assignment and Initialization Are Different* [12, 41]:

```
String names[] = { "my", "dog", "has", "fleece" };
const int namesLen = sizeof(names)/sizeof(names[0]);
slowSort( names, namesLen ); // sorts...eventually!
```

The first complaint one might make concerning `slowSort` is that it can be slow. That observation is correct, but let's forgive `slowSort` its $O(n^2)$ runtime and concentrate instead on aspects of its generic design.

The first observation we can make is that our implementation of swap in `slowSort` is not ideal for the `String` type (or many other types, for that matter). The `String` class has its own member `swap` that is both faster and more exception safe than a swap that is accomplished by copying through a temporary `String`. A better implementation approach is simply to say what we mean:

```
template <typename T>
void slowSort( T a[], int len ) {
    for( int i = 0; i < len; ++i ) // For each pair
        for( int j = i; j < len; ++j )
            if( a[j] < a[i] ) // ...if out of order...
                swap( a[j], a[i] ); // ...swap them.
}
```

We're still not calling `String`'s `swap` member function, but if the author of the `String` class has it together, there will be a nonmember `swap` available that will:

```
inline void swap( String &a, String &b )
    { a.swap( b ); }
```

Suppose there is no such nonmember `swap` available? In that case, we'll be no worse off because one way or another we'll end up calling the standard library `swap`, which does precisely the same thing we hand-coded in the original version of `slowSort`. Actually, we're still much better off than we were originally, because the new implementation of `slowSort` is shorter, simpler, and easier to understand. More important, if someone should eventually implement an efficient nonmember `swap` for `String`, we'll pick up the improvement automatically. That's the kind of code maintenance we can live with.

Now consider the use of < for comparing elements of the array. This is probably the most common way one would like to sort an array (from smallest to largest), but we may also want to sort in descending order or in some idiosyncratic order. Further, there may be arrays of objects we'd like to sort that either don't support a < operator or have several distinct candidates for a less-than-like operator. We've already seen such a type in *STL Function Objects* [20, 71]: the `State` class:

```
class State {
  public:
```

```
    //...
    int population() const;
    float aveTempF() const;
    //...
};
```

Our approach in *STL Function Objects* [20, 71] was to implement functions and function objects that could be used in place of a < operator, but this approach will work only if the generic algorithm has been designed to accept such an argument:

```
template <typename T, typename Comp>
void slowSort( T a[], int len, Comp less ) {
    for( int i = 0; i < len; ++i ) // For each pair
        for( int j = i; j < len; ++j )
            if( less( a[j], a[i] ) ) // ...if out of order...
                swap( a[j], a[i] ); // ...swap them.
}
//...
State states[50];
//...
slowSort( states, 50, PopComp() );
```

If `slowSorting` with < is a very common operation, it might be a good idea to overload `slowSort` so that it can be called either with or without a special purpose comparison operation.

Finally, it's always a good idea to follow convention, and it's a particularly good idea in the case of generic algorithms. We can also justifiably criticize `slowSort` for restricting the argument it sorts to be an array, since there are many other kinds of containers or data structures that we might like to sort. When in doubt, copy the standard:

```
template <typename For, typename Comp>
void slowSort(For b, For e, Comp less) {
    for(For i( b ); i != e; ++i )
        for(For j( i ); j != e; ++j )
            if( less( *j, *i ) )
                std::swap( *j, *i );
}
```

```
template <typename For>
void slowSort(For b, For e) {
    for(For i( b ); i != e; ++i )
        for(For j( i ); j != e ; ++j )
            if( *j < *i )
                std::swap( *j, *i );
}
//...
std::list<State> states;
//...
slowSort( states.begin(), states.end(), PopComp() );
slowSort( names, names+namesLen );
```

Here we've replaced our clunky array interface with a more standard and more flexible STL compliant iterator interface. Now we can feel comfortable calling `slowSort` a generic algorithm, rather than simply a function template.

One important lesson of this example is that complex software design is nearly always a group effort. As such, your code should be designed in such a way as to leverage the expertise of your colleagues while remaining as immune as possible to maintenance they perform on code that is not in your control. Our improved `slowSort` algorithm is a good example of such proper design. It performs a single, well-understood operation at as high a conceptual level as possible. To be precise, `slowSort` handles the sorting algorithm and subcontracts swapping and comparison to others who will do a better job. This approach allows you, the (supposed) sorting expert, to augment your sorting expertise with the swapping expertise of whoever designed the element type that is being sorted. The two of you may never meet, but through proper design you can work together as closely as if you shared the same workstation. Moreover, if improved swap functionality should appear in the future, `slowSort` will pick up the improvement automatically and probably without your knowledge. As ever, ignorance is strength. (This is similar in flavor to proper polymorphic design; see *Commands and Hollywood* [19, 67].)

Item 61 You Instantiate What You Use

In both C and C++, if you don't call a declared function (or take its address), you don't have to define it. An analogous situation occurs with member functions of class templates; if you don't actually call a template's member function, it's not instantiated.

This is clearly a handy property for the purpose of reducing code size. If a class template defines a large number of member functions, but you use only two or three of them, you don't pay the code space penalty for all those unused functions.

An even more important result of this rule is that you can specialize class templates with arguments that would be illegal if all the member functions were instantiated. With this rule in place, it's possible to write flexible class templates that can work with a wide variety of arguments, even if some arguments would result in erroneous instantiations of some member functions; if you don't actually call those erroneous functions, they're not instantiated, and you don't get an error. This is consistent with many areas of the C++ language, where potential problems are not flagged as errors until they become actual problems. In C++, it's OK to think illegal thoughts as long as you don't act on them!

Consider a simple, fixed-size array template:

```
template <typename T, int n>
class Array {
  public:
    Array() : a_( new T[n] ) {}
    ~Array() { delete [] a_; }
    Array( const Array & );
    Array &operator =( const Array & );
    void swap( Array &that ) { std::swap( a_, that.a_ ); }
    T &operator []( int i ) { return a_[i]; }
    const T &operator []( int i ) const { return a_[i]; }
```

```
    bool operator ==( const Array &rhs ) const;
    bool operator !=( const Array &rhs ) const
        { return !(*this==rhs); }
  private:
    T *a_;
};
```

This container behaves pretty much like a predefined array, with the usual operations for indexing, but it also provides some higher-level operations that are not available on predefined arrays, like swapping and comparison for equality (we've left out the relational operators for reasons of space). Let's look at an implementation of `operator ==`:

```
template <typename T, int n>
bool Array<T,n>::operator ==( const Array &that ) const {
    for( int i = 0; i < n; ++i )
        if( !(a_[i] == that.a_[i]) )
            return false;
    return true;
}
```

We know that both arrays being compared have the same number of elements, since they're both the same type and the array size is one of the template parameters, so we just have to perform a pairwise comparison of each element. If any pair of elements differs, the `Array` objects are not equal.

```
Array<int,12> a, b;
//...
if( a == b ) // calls a.operator ==(b)
    //...
```

When we use the == operation on our `Array<int,12>` objects, the compiler instantiates `Array<int,12>::operator ==`, which compiles correctly. If we hadn't used == (or `!=`, which calls `operator ==`) on objects of type `Array<int,12>`, then we would not have instantiated that member function.

The interesting situation occurs when we instantiate `Array` with a type that does not have an == operation defined. For instance, let's assume that our `Circle` type does not define or inherit an `operator ==`:

```
Array<Circle,6> c, d; // no problem!
//...
c[3].draw(); // OK
```

So far, so good. We have not directly or indirectly used an == operation on an `Array<Circle,6>` object, so the `operator ==` function is not instantiated, and there is no error.

```
if( c == d ) // error!
```

Now we have a problem. The compiler will attempt to instantiate `Array<Circle,6>::operator ==`, but the function implementation will attempt to compare two `Circle` objects with a nonexistent == operator. Compile-time error.

This technique is commonly used in the design of class templates that are as flexible as possible but no more so.

Note that this idyllic situation does not occur in the case of an explicit instantiation of a class template:

```
template Array<Circle,7>; // error!
```

This explicit instantiation directive tells the compiler to instantiate `Array` and all its members with the arguments `Circle` and `7`, resulting in a compile-time error in the instantiation of `Array<Circle,7>::operator ==`. Well, you asked for it....

Item 62 Include Guards

Production C++ applications tend to use a lot of header files, and many header files include other header files. Under these circumstances, it's common for the same header file to be indirectly included more than once in a compilation, and it's not uncommon in large, complex applications for the same header file to occur hundreds of times in the same compilation. Consider the simple case of a header file `hdr2.h` that includes another header file, `hdr1.h`, and a header file `hdr3.h` that also includes `hdr1.h`. If both `hdr2.h` and `hdr3.h` are included in the same source file, `hdr1.h` will be included twice. Typically, such multiple inclusions are undesirable and cause multiple definition errors.

For this reason, C++ header files almost universally employ a preprocessor coding technique to prevent the content of the header from appearing more than once in a compilation no matter how many times the header file is actually `#included`. Consider the content of header file `hdr1.h`:

```
#ifndef HDR1_H
#define HDR1_H
// actual content of the header file...
#endif
```

The first time the header file `hdr1.h` is `#included` in a compilation, the preprocessor symbol `HDR1_H` is undefined, so the `#ifndef` ("if not defined") preprocessor conditional allows preprocessing of the `#define` directive and the rest of the header file's content. The next time `hdr1.h` appears in the same compilation, the symbol `HDR1_H` is defined, and the `#ifndef` prevents repeated inclusion of the header file's content.

This technique will work only if the preprocessor symbol for a header file (in this case, `HDR1_H`) is associated with exactly one header file (in this case, `hdr1.h`). It's therefore important to establish a standard, simple naming convention that allows the construction of the name of the preprocessor symbol used in the include guard from the name of the header file being guarded.

In addition to preventing error, include file guards also help to speed up compilation by allowing the compiler to skip over the content of any header files that have already been translated. Unfortunately, the very process of opening a header file, evaluating the #ifndef, and scanning to the terminating #endif can be time-consuming in complex situations where many header files appear many times in a given compilation. In some cases, redundant include guards can speed things up considerably:

```
#ifndef HDR1_H
#include "hdr1.h"
#endif
```

Rather than simply #include a header file, we guard the inclusion with a test on the same guard symbol that is set within the header file. This is redundant, because the first time a header file is included, the same condition (in this case, #ifndef HDR1_H) will be tested twice, both before the #include and within the header file itself. However, on subsequent inclusions, the redundant guard will prevent the #include directive from being executed, preventing the header file from being needlessly opened and scanned. Use of redundant include guards is not as common as that of simple include guards, but in some cases their use can improve compilation times of large applications considerably.

Item 63 | Optional Keywords

Some keyword usage is strictly optional from the perspective of the C++ language, though other considerations may argue for their presence or absence.

The most common source of confusion is the optional use of `virtual` in a derived class member function that overrides a base class virtual member function.

```
class Shape {
  public:
    virtual void draw() const = 0;
    virtual void rotate( double degrees ) = 0;
    virtual void invert() = 0;
    //...
};
class Blob : public Shape {
  public:
    virtual void draw() const;
    void rotate( double );
    void invert() = 0;
    //...
};
```

The member function `Blob::draw` overrides the base class `draw` function and so is virtual; the use of the keyword is completely optional and has no effect on the meaning of the program. A common misassumption is that omitting the `virtual` keyword will prevent further overriding in more derived classes. This is not the case.

```
class SharpBlob : public Blob {
  public:
    void rotate( double ); // overrides Blob::rotate
    //...
};
```

Note that the appearance of the `virtual` keyword is also optional on an overriding pure virtual function, as in `Blob::invert`. The presence or absence of the `virtual` keyword in an overriding derived class function is completely optional and has no effect on the meaning of the program. None.

Opinion is divided as to whether it is a good practice to omit the `virtual` keyword in an overriding derived class function. Some authorities claim that use of the nonessential `virtual` helps to document the nature of the derived class function for the human reader. Others claim it's a waste of effort and may cause a nonoverriding derived class function to become "accidentally" virtual. No matter which opinion you hold, it is best to be consistent; either use the `virtual` keyword on every overriding derived class function or omit its use entirely.

The `static` keyword is optional when declaring member `operator new`, `operator delete`, array new, and array delete (see *Class-Specific Memory Management* [36, 123]), because these functions are implicitly static.

```
class Handle {
  public:
    void *operator new( size_t ); // implicitly static
    static void operator delete( void * );
    static void *operator new[]( size_t );
    void operator delete[]( void * ); // implicitly static
};
```

Some authorities claim that it's best to be specific and always declare these functions to be explicitly static. Others think that if a user or maintainer of a piece of C++ does not know these functions are implicitly static, they should not be using or maintaining the code. The use of `static` here is a waste of effort; a program is no place to put crib notes on language semantics. As with the optional use of `virtual`, whatever your position on optional `static`, it's important to be consistent. Either all four of these functions should be declared explicitly static or none of them should.

In a template header, the keywords `typename` and `class` may be used interchangeably to indicate that a template parameter is a type name; there is no difference in meaning whatsoever. However, many expert C++ programmers use `typename` to indicate to the human reader that the template argument may be of any type and `class` to indicate that the type argument must be a class type.

```
template <typename In, typename Out>
Out copy( In begin, In end, Out result );

template <class Container>
void resize( Container &container, int newSize );
```

In ancient times, the `register` keyword was used to "suggest" to the compiler that a variable was (in the opinion of the programmer) going to be heavily used and should be therefore be put in a register. It was also illegal to take the address of a variable declared with the `register` storage class. Early on, however, compiler writers learned that their programming colleagues were absolutely clueless about what variables should be stored in registers, and now compilers uniformly ignore programmers' suggestions in that regard. In C++, use of `register` has no effect whatsoever on the meaning of the program and typically has no effect on the efficiency of the program.

The `auto` keyword can be used to indicate that an automatic variable (a function argument or a local variable) is automatic. Don't bother with it.

To be perfectly honest, both `register` and `auto` can be used in obscure circumstances to disambiguate the syntax of particularly poorly written code. The proper approach in these cases is to write better code and avoid use of these keywords.

Bibliography

Alexandrescu, Andrei. *Modern C++ Design*. Addison-Wesley, 2001.

Dewhurst, Stephen C. *C++ Gotchas*. Addison-Wesley, 2003.

Gamma, Erich, Richard Helm, Ralph Johnson, and John Vlissides. *Design Patterns*. Addison-Wesley, 1995.

Josuttis, Nicolai M. *The C++ Standard Library*. Addison-Wesley, 1999.

Meyers, Scott. *Effective C++*, Third Edition. Addison-Wesley, 2005.

———. *Effective STL*. Addison-Wesley, 2001.

———. *More Effective C++*. Addison-Wesley, 1996.

Sutter, Herb. *Exceptional C++*. Addison-Wesley, 2000.

———. *More Exceptional C++*. Addison-Wesley, 2002.

———. *Exceptional C++Style*. Addison-Wesley, 2005.

Sutter, Herb, and Andrei Alexandrescu. *C++ Coding Standards*. Addison-Wesley, 2005.

Vandevoorde, David, and Nicolai M. Josuttis. *C++ Templates*. Addison-Wesley, 2003.

Wilson, Matthew. *Imperfect C++*. Addison-Wesley, 2005.

Index

See also Index of Code Examples, page 245

C

J

K

L

M

N

O

Index of Code Examples

See also Index, page 237

A

B

C

D

E

I

M

N

O

P

W

X

Z

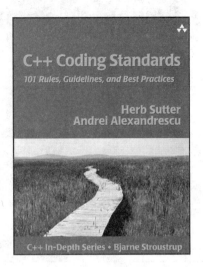

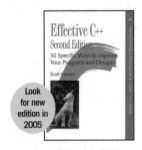

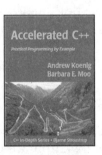